Praise for *Mid-Career Crisis*

"Jean [Russell Nave] has mastered a topic that has a wide variety of applications. From individuals desiring a career change to those who have been trapped in a company through years of promotion who truly need a career change. She has demonstrated her skills in her professionalism and has effectively translated that knowledge and enthusiasm into a valuable resource tool for all of us."

—Randy C. James, Chairman and CEO
Bank of America, Oregon

"The key in this book is how it helps the reader evaluate personal values. Then it opens their eyes to see the future opportunities and options available."

—Mark Wickert, Senior Account Manager
AT&T (Paradyne)

"As a manager of a large and diverse department, [I believe] this book provides insight into how to counsel the many people who are going through, or in the future may go through, a mid-career crisis."

—Tom Cook, General Credit Manager
Nike, Inc.

"Not enough people spend enough time thinking about their values and what keeps them happy and motivated. The authors walk you through a process to assess where you are and where you might go. The step-by-step process makes you feel better about yourself and what may be of more value to you."

—Ron B. Gould, Partner, Tax Services
Deloitte & Touche

"This book includes great tools for hands-on techniques to determine an individual's market worth."

—Eugene E. Holt, Financial Consultant
Merrill Lynch

"This book covers all the basics for mastering a mid-career crisis. Its personal and real-world approach provides guidance and help to affected managers. The techniques for self-evaluation and the requirements for career success guide the reader in critical career decision-making. The chapters on self-marketing alone make it invaluable to businessmen and women."

—Dulany Foster, Jr., Senior Vice President
Korn/Ferry International

Mid-Career Crisis

Jean Russell Nave and
Louise M. Nelson

FOREWORD BY F. G. "BUCK" RODGERS

A PERIGEE BOOK

Perigee Books
are published by
The Putnam Publishing Group
200 Madison Avenue
New York, NY 10016

Copyright © 1991 by Jean Russell Nave and Louise M. Nelson

All rights reserved. This book, or parts thereof,
may not be reproduced in any form without permission.
Published simultaneously in Canada

Library of Congress Cataloging-in-Publication Data

Nave, Jean Russell, date.
    Mid-career crisis / by Jean Russell Nave, Louise M. Nelson; foreword
by F. G. "Buck" Rodgers.
        p.   cm.
    "A Perigee book."
    ISBN 0-399-51683-2
        1. Career changes—United States.   2. Occupational mobility—
United States.   I. Nelson, Louise M., date.   II. Title.
HF5384.N38   1991   91-16310 CIP
650.14—dc20

Cover design by Antler & Baldwin Design Group

Printed in the United States of America
        2   3   4   5   6   7   8   9   10

In memory of our mother and father,
Gale P. Bartlett and Carolyn M. Bartlett,
in appreciation for teaching the value
of ingenuity and the power of persistence

Contents

Acknowledgments

MANY PEOPLE gave us aid and comfort during our year-long effort to complete *Mid-Career Crisis*. A heartfelt thanks to everyone who helped us in one way or another.

With the kiss of this book's very special godmother, our editor Judy Linden, a frog of a manuscript was transformed into a prince of a book.

Special thanks to Andy Nelson and Robert Russell for their thoughtful criticisms, insightful contributions, and constant challenges, which steered us toward accuracy and completion.

Thanks to our "readers" who told us what we were doing right and where we needed to improve: Bob Kipe, Rick Pay, Rebecca Crimmins, and Mark Wickert. Mary C. Pauli of Clackamas County (OR) Library must be thanked for her help in locating statistics and background materials.

Finally, thanks to two special people who believed in us and helped make this book possible: F. G. "Buck" Rodgers, our friend; and Natasha Kern, our agent.

Foreword

A CAREER CHANGE, whether by desire or by necessity, offers you a chance to evaluate what is important to you, in your career and in your personal life. If you face it with self-confidence, you will find a new place where your contribution will be well rewarded and your quality of life improved.

The majority of white-collar workers drift into their careers. This is leaving an awful lot to luck considering that next to your family, the company you work for becomes your most important and valued relationship.

Success at your career depends in part on the reality of your expectations. Your expectations are affected by how well you analyze yourself and how much you research the prospective career opportunity you choose to pursue.

Several years ago I embarked on a second career. After taking early retirement from IBM, where I had been corporate vice president of marketing, I entered the uncertain world of motivational speaking and writing. This change required a great amount of soul-searching as well as establishing new priorities. That review helped me see the challenges and opportunities in a clear light.

As you pursue a career change, do not expect a magical solution to all of your problems and challenges, and do not expect a change to come without effort and sacrifice. Things of value require good old-fashioned hard work and a commitment to excellence. However, when you succeed, then it all becomes worthwhile.

Best of luck,
F. G. "Buck" Rodgers

Buck Rodgers is the author of several best-selling books, including *The IBM Way* and *Getting the Best Out of Yourself and Others*.

Introduction

THIS BOOK was written from experience. Both we and our husbands have successfully recovered from a mid-career crisis—a professional mid-life crisis of sorts. As professional speakers and consultants, we have helped hundreds of clients and numerous friends through the pain, agony, and ultimate transformation experienced when the decision is made to change careers.

Experience taught us a lot. We learned that you need to know two key items found in this book: 1) the quantified assessment of your transferable skills; and 2) the accurate value of those skills on the open job market. These are not found in any other book.

There is more. In Chapter 1 you learn that your problem is **mid-career syndrome,** a recoverable state of depression and disillusionment. In Chapter 2 you get an accurate assessment of **how much time you have to plan** a career change. Chapter 3 identifies the probable main cause of your mid-career syndrome: a conflict in values. Chapters 4 and 5 show you how to change careers and **retain your career equity,** the money value of your skills and experience. A table then gives you **logical career options,** their cost, and the required effort to achieve success.

Chapter 6 may be the main **reason you are reading this book.** It contains a set of twenty-seven Skills Market Value Charts & Worksheets. These charts offer you an opportunity to determine how equitable your current pay is and **how much you can expect to earn** if you change jobs or careers. The results give you new insight into any job or career change you are contemplating.

Chapter 7 addresses a question we are constantly asked. **How and where can a mid-career changer get help?** This chapter gives simple, direct, and complete answers.

Chapters 8 and 9 deal with the unique problem a mid-career changer faces, **deciding what career change is best.** We give you a way to assess the option of going into business for yourself. We also explore the advantages and disadvantages of different business sectors. People who have spent their career in one sector usually know little about another. We never found a source that dealt with these issues, so we wrote one ourselves.

Chapters 10, 11, and 12 can be found in other career books, but those books do not address the *specific* needs of a mid-career changer. What is important to a recent college graduate and what is important to an individual fifteen years into a career are not necessarily the same. The experienced mid-career changer has valuable skills that have to be carefully displayed and promoted so they retain career equity when transferred to another career field.

This book gives you the essential information you need to successfully complete your journey through a mid-career crisis. When you finish reading it, you will have a better understanding of yourself, and a greater appreciation for those out there who can help you on your way.

Chapter 1

Mid-Career Crisis— A Fact in Today's Career World

WHEN WE WERE YOUNG, most of us had a dream. It went like this . . . Go to a good school, get the right degree, and find a great-paying job. Then, with our career secured, we'd be home free. Work hard and we'd get consistent raises, a nice home, a new car, and an assured retirement. Today that dream is as much a fantasy as "The Adventures of Ozzie and Harriet." In its place are fear, job stress, and sometimes unemployment.

What happened to the dream? Many things. Running a business in the United States really is more difficult than it used to be. Today corporate managers fight the Goliath of global competition, who slashes profits right and left. Markets change or disappear before their eyes. New technology obsoletes products overnight. And on top of all of this, rolling recessions whipsaw interest rates, prices, and material availability. Today, management's tools for survival are down-sizing, streamlining, and imposing hiring freezes.

Clint, a manager of finance when he came to us, remembers the cold June evening in 1984 when he came home, flicked on "The Nightly Business Report," and was stunned to hear that the food processing company for which he worked had just been acquired by a private investor. His $70,000-a-year job was eliminated within weeks. No one cared that he'd been rated "superior" on his last job evaluation. Nor did his twenty-three years with the company mean anything. The new owner said to him and thousands of others, "Hit the road, you're out!" The company's New Jersey corporate headquarters went from 5,000 employees to less than 125 in two years.

According to *The Wall Street Journal*, an estimated 3 million middle managers lost their jobs in the 1980s, yet blue-collar jobs in the manufacturing sector took the brunt of layoffs during that decade. Tough times are not over. The 1990s started with an estimated loss of 300,000 jobs in the first year. Some statistics indicate that 70 percent of the cuts were white-collar workers. Most of those were supervisors, managers, or professionals. People have found that good credentials and hard work aren't enough to dodge the unemployment rolls.

"When I graduated from college, my father had a friend that got me an interview with the food processing company," says Clint. "Dad believed I would be set for life by getting that job. If he could see what happened, he'd be shocked."

We asked Clint if he'd seen the takeover coming. "Everyone knew the company's profits were down," he said. "We knew there were undervalued assets on the books, but the company was so big, we really didn't think anyone would buy it."

Clint was lucky. With help, he started a new career in less than six months. He became a stockbroker, something he had thought about for years. The shock and disillusionment of losing his job made him strike out in a new direction. However, his story didn't end there. Two years as a stockbroker gave him a new appreciation for the security of a regular paycheck and he began a quiet search for a chief financial officer position. His connections as a broker gave him an edge.

In three months he landed a CFO position with a $60-million manufacturing firm.

How does he feel about his job security now? "I've learned a lot over the past few years. I no longer believe in the dream of retiring with a comfortable pension from any one company. I don't speculate in the market; I buy blue chip stocks to build my own retirement program. I have a new sense about controlling my own destiny. I'll work hard for my boss, with the knowledge that he can let me go in a heartbeat. And I'm prepared."

What Is Mid-Career Syndrome and Why Has It Developed?

The average person falls into a career. Once they leave school they job hop for a short time and finally find one that pays well, is in the right location, or has opportunities for advancement. Most people end up working for ABC International Widget Company, buried in a department doing something they don't like. That was not their dream in the beginning; the ideal career got lost.

A mid-career crisis strikes people who have worked fifteen to twenty years at a job and cannot face another fifteen to twenty doing the same thing. Or they may lose their job unexpectedly. Whatever the reason, with school tuitions, mortgage payments, and doctor bills to pay, they feel it is almost impossible to make a change. They feel stuck.

Career dislocation or dissatisfaction is not the only problem. Feeling trapped and frustrated makes some people lash out at their family. They lose the support of spouse and children at a time when they need it most. This loss can cause depression. That simply makes things worse. We call these combined symptoms *mid-career syndrome*.

Most who suffer mid-career syndrome have had a successful career up to that point. They look around, see how well they have done, and think they *should* be satisfied with what they have. The fact that they are not satisfied makes them feel guilty, and this exacerbates their depression.

When some people lose their job they say, "If I were *really* good, I'd still have that job!" They see others still working and begin making comparisons. They dwell on their short-comings, convincing themselves that something is wrong with *them*. Succumbing to these feelings of guilt and inadequacy leads to a loss of confidence and to low self-esteem . . . again compounding depression.

Individuals who cure mid-career syndrome learn how to see the impending change as an opportunity to make a fresh start. They see a chance for a new beginning to the second half of their life, and become determined to do better for themselves with this new opportunity.

The Typical Mid-Career Syndrome Candidate

We have identified three main groups of people suffering from mid-career syndrome: **dislocated** or fired workers; **burned-out** individuals; and employees whose **career skills** have become **obsolete.**

Clint typifies the **dislocated** mid-career manager. He was forty-five years old when the ax fell (the average age is thirty-five to fifty), he'd been with his company for more than twenty years (average is fifteen to twenty), and he earned a good living (average is $35,000 a year or more). Once fired, he did a very common thing, too; he changed career fields.

Our experience as career consultants indicates that about 50 percent of the mid-career job changers do more than change companies or industries. Like Clint, they find new careers altogether. That's generally why they come to us. They need guidance transferring their valued skills into new career fields.

If Clint hadn't been fired, it was only a matter of time before he would have come to us anyway. He was **burned-out.** He hated Mondays. He counted the days until Friday. He went home early any day he had a chance. His homelife was falling apart, and his health was declining.

These symptoms are classic of the second group of people with mid-career syndrome. Somewhere between ages thirty-five and fifty (the age range of a group of people fondly known today as baby-boomers), many Americans find life getting more complicated and less rewarding instead of simpler and more satisfying. At 6:30 A.M. each Monday, when the alarm sounds, they find it takes everything they have just to face another day at the office. But they're trapped. There are so many bills to pay. They believe they have to keep their job. Everyone has heard the horror story "Joe was out of work for two years." Fear and paralysis set in. They know they'd never be able to find another job with a paycheck large enough to keep up their life-style.

The average mid-career syndrome candidate has not had a real interview in fifteen years or more. He doesn't know where to begin a job search. He hasn't written a resume since leaving college. Besides, how could he look for a job without his boss finding out?

A recent Gallup poll surveying employee attitudes found that one third of the people questioned expected to leave their job within the next three years. A spokesperson for the pollster said, "The results of the poll indicate a large number of Americans feel trapped in their jobs."

There are 116 million people employed in the United States. Baby-boomers dominate that employment pool. Many of these people—a growing number every day—have mid-career syndrome. Early in their careers they expected to have it all. They wanted more than the old American dream of a chicken in every pot and a car in every garage. They wanted two chickens in their pot and three cars in their garage. To afford that, both partners had to work; and after years of such a pace, many people found the price was too high for this new American dream. They expected material possessions to make them happy. But once they had a nice house, three cars, and four televisions, they still wanted something else. They wanted fulfillment. They desired the love and respect of their family, they needed to make a valued contribution in their work, and they craved the satisfaction of making a difference in their community. Sixty-hour work weeks coupled with big-city commutes have left little or no time for any of these.

The third, and smallest, group of people suffering from mid-career syndrome are those whose **career skills** are becoming **obsolete.** They find themselves in a changing world of technology but can't keep up. These people suffer extreme anxiety at the thought of cozying up to a computer. They believe in the axiom "If it ain't broke, don't fix it." They managed well enough without the dumb things, so why do they have to use one now? For a few years they were able to avoid technology in the workplace. But too much has happened. Today they have to change or leave.

Regardless of the cause of mid-career syndrome, we have learned that these common symptoms have a common set of cures.

Getting a Handle on Mid-Career Syndrome

On the Richter scale of anxiety, job change or job loss rates nearly as high as coping with the death of a close family member. Stress from mid-career syndrome can be a potent and pervasive toxin that affects your health. Left untreated, the stress symptoms can sabotage your future success.

Through the years we have learned a few simple tricks to help deal with the symptoms of mid-career syndrome. These symptoms fall into three primary groups:

1. Depression
2. Withdrawal from family and friends
3. The grass-is-greener delusion

1. Coping with Depression

The fundamental cause of depression is a negative attitude. It is a feeling of hopelessness, a belief that nothing can go right. Very few people with mid-career syndrome escape feeling depressed at some point.

Richard had been the service manager for a utility-truck manufacturer. Overseas competition cut a deep hole in the company's profits, and at fifty-two years of age Richard became a casualty. His job search resulted in door after door being slammed in his face. Never mind the laws against age discrimination. In reality, career transition past age fifty is difficult. Richard came to us after nine months of unemployment. He was desperate. We reviewed his marketing plan, brushed up his resume, and coached him on interviewing. This made no difference. His depression oozed from his pores. You could see it the minute he walked into the room. His age was an obstacle, but his attitude was a barrier. He believed he could not afford a psychological counselor, so we shared our attitude-building tip with him. In thirty days he was carrying his head higher; in ninety days he had a new career.

Here's our tip. Buy a 3″ × 5″ spiral notebook. Each night before you go to bed, list three things that went well—three wins—during the day. It does not matter how small the victories are. If you had a really lousy day, maybe your first entry is nothing more than, "I remembered to pick up my win book and write something in it."

Do this every day for at least thirty days. As time goes on, read the notes from previous days. Notice the consistent increase in the positive quality of the entries. Keeping a win book creates and reinforces the habit of noticing the good things that are happening in your life. The more you notice the positive things happening around you, the easier it becomes to take advantage of opportunities. If your sight is clouded by a negative fog, you won't see an opportunity that is right in front of your face. Your win book can bring out the sun.

2. Preventing Withdrawal

Even though it may sometimes seem otherwise, your family cares about your career, your happiness, and your success. Too often people struggling with mid-career syndrome withdraw from their family rather than seek their support. During this difficult time it is imperative that you build solid communication bridges.

If you have never been one to discuss your inner feelings with your spouse, now is the time to begin. If you are like most people who fear openness, you are afraid that revealing yourself will show others your weaknesses, imperfections, and uncertainties. Although this does happen, you both must share your feelings in order to have a healthy relationship.

Your family needs to understand why you are having problems with your present situation and why you need a change. Discuss with them how your job is frustrating. Help them understand the effect your frustration has on your current homelife. Discuss how things could be better if you were able to change jobs or careers. Through active listening, gain their perspective, find out what is important to them. Explore what impact different career scenarios would have on the lives of your spouse and your children. The resulting understanding will help your family cope with the disruption your career change will bring.

Try this approach: when you first come home from work, set aside a few minutes each day, about half an hour, to talk quietly with your spouse. If you have children, tell them that Mom and Dad need fifteen to thirty minutes of quiet. Encourage them to play outside or in their rooms. Use this special time to share the good things that have happened to each of you during the day. Make a special effort to express feelings of love, understanding, and support for each other. Be sure this is a positive time; deal with problems later. If you make this a habit, in a year you will find that you not only successfully changed careers but also strengthened your marriage in the process.

3. Checking the Grass-Is-Greener Delusion

The grass is always greener on the other side of the fence. When your ground is hard and dry, your neighbor's is moist and lush. Right? Maybe, but probably not. It is true that we are now living in a time of rolling recessions. During the 1980s when the Northeast was in a boom, the Northwest was in severe recession. During the early 1990s, when the Northeast saw its economic bubble burst, the Northwest was still bubbling along at top boil. So depending upon which coast you were on at what time, you could say others had it better than you. Yet in each region at any given time, some people were prospering and others were not. Why the difference?

To a large extent we make our luck. As consultants, we've sat and listened to one person after another tell us how terrible the job market is, only to learn that they made one or two calls *a week* on prospective employers. Other people would come to us working on the same type of career change and land a new job in two months. These individuals developed a marketing plan that included the task of making five to ten prospect calls *a day*. They worked the plan and it paid off in "good luck."

Clint was a good example of someone with the grass-is-greener delusion. He thought being a stockbroker would be a cinch. He loved the market and made numerous trades on a weekly basis. Once he became a broker, he found that "cold calling" on the telephone was the biggest part of his job. "I used to do a war dance around the telephone just getting up the courage to make another phone call," he remembers. The job wasn't nearly as much fun as he thought it would be.

Why did he misjudge it so? Because even though he interviewed a few brokers before he applied, he listened only to the "good stuff" they told him. He switched his hearing off when the discussion touched on areas that were difficult or distasteful, because he had already made up his mind that a broker's job was better than what he had been doing before. He asked the questions, but he did not listen to the answers.

The antidote for this problem is objectivity. Realize that there are problems as well as positive aspects of any job. Work at listening to everything, not just what you want to hear, to ensure you don't get caught in the grass-is-greener delusion.

The Next Step

Mid-career syndrome is not fatal. The symptoms can be treated, but the cure will take time. You need to keep a positive attitude and enlist the help and support of your family and friends, and you must be committed to the effort required to properly assess and pursue your new career.

Chapter 2

How Secure Is Your Job?

WE HAVE ALL MET the dentist who dreamed of being an Egyptologist, or the engineer who wanted to be a mystery writer. Most people are not looking for such a dramatic career change, but a sizable number indicate a desire to change their line of work. In a recent *Newsweek* magazine poll, 62 percent of the respondents said they would change their career field if they were to lose their current job. To succeed at such an undertaking, an individual must have a well-thought-out plan. Formulating a workable plan requires a good deal of information, the first piece being an accurate assessment of *time*. You must know how much time you have to prepare for the transition.

Measuring Your Job Security

Provided someone has not already handed you a pink slip, how is your opportunity to assess your job's stability and determine how much time you have to plan and execute your next career move. To do this, you need to know *how secure your current job is.*

The chart at the end of this chapter offers you a quick guide. It is based upon five primary factors that influence job security:

1. The **industry** in which you work
2. The **region** in which you live
3. The **profession** you have chosen
4. The **size** of the **company** for which you work
5. The amount and kind of **education** you have

Several elements and subelements affect each one of these factors, as you will see on the chart. Use the chart as a guide. It is possible that something else could affect your job security even though it is not reflected on the chart. If you know about it, consider its influence upon the results you compute. The more data you can gather to help quantify how much time you have for planning and executing your career change, the better off you will be.

The balance of this chapter is dedicated to explaining each element and subelement of the chart. Once you have read the explanations, you should be able to use the chart to compute your own job security and to gain an understanding of what really affects the security of a job. Be sure to read this entire chapter *before* you do your computation; we want to be sure you understand what each subelement means and whether or not you should circle it. Otherwise your computation could be inaccurate.

Weighting the Subelements in the Chart

As you look at the chart, you will notice that each subelement has a number to its left. When you use the chart, you will circle the appropriate subelements. Their numbers will be added together to determine the security of your job. The lower the total, the more secure your job is. The numbers are weighted, which means that each subelement may have a different weight or impact upon your job security. For example, the subelement "Transportation" under the heading "Manufacturing" has a weighted number of 10. A 10 is also next to the subelement "Poor Profitability" under the heading "Small," relating to company size. This means that both subelements have the same relative impact on your job's stability when compared with the impact of all other subelements within the table.

Notice that the weighted number is lower for the subelement "Poor Profitability" under the heading "Medium," and still lower for "Poor Profitability" under the heading "Large." The weighted impact of profitability goes down as company size increases. The bigger a company is, the longer it can sustain an operating loss. For example, you may read that Ford Motor Company announces a quarterly loss of hundreds of millions of dollars. In spite of the announced loss, the company will keep going. By contrast, ABC Widget International Company, whose annual sales are $15 million, may not be able to keep its doors open for a week if it loses $1 million in a quarter. If profits are down or your company is incurring quarterly operating losses, your job security is affected according to the overall size of the company.

The weighted numbers have been computed by comparing each factor to all others and analyzing unemployment statistics. Then each element was weighted against our knowledge of the methods used by management to determine whom to lay off and whom to keep.

Defining the Elements That Affect Your Job Security

Following is an explanation of the five primary factors, including their elements and subelements. Pay close attention to these items and their definitions. Each item on the chart is directed at a *specific* job-security issue. Don't try to read more into the definition than is intended. Remember, the lower your score, the more secure your job is. Don't try to read between the lines—you should circle only what *is* on the chart and what applies directly to your job. It is okay *not* to circle a subelement. Work the chart *after* you have read this chapter.

If you follow the instructions and carefully read each explanation, you will be able to compute an accurate score.

1. Industry

Within the category of industry, three elements are cited: manufacturing, service, and retail. Circle a subelement in this category only if your job is within one of the specifically mentioned industries.

Manufacturing took the brunt of the layoffs during the 1980s. As a result, only the three manufacturing groups mentioned on the chart are having major downsizing problems today. If your industry does not appear on the chart, you are probably fairly secure. Apparel, electronics, and transportation are still having problems, primarily due to global competition and high U.S. wages. These challenging problems are not expected to improve in the near future.

Service businesses are the fastest growing sector in the American business economy. Yet some areas are having problems. If one of these areas represents your industry, circle the appropriate line.

The 1980s saw an enormous rush toward building nursing homes, expanding hospitals, and developing off-site immediate-care facilities. But cuts in government spending and turmoil over skyrocketing insurance costs have caused severe reductions in demand. This has resulted in major layoffs of medical services personnel.

Travel and entertainment, since they rely on discretionary income, can be easily affected by recession. We are not yet through the rolling recessions, so this industry sector will regionally expand and contract, making job security tenuous at times. If you work in this business sector, pay close attention to how busy your company is. If the place is slow and has been for a while, your time in the job could be limited, depending upon the influence of the other subelements you circle on the chart.

Financial institutions, including banks, savings and loan associations, and insurance companies, are having a very difficult time. If you lose your job in this industry, you may find that a career change is mandatory rather than optional.

Experts predict this industry will have problems far into the 1990s.

Retail, like travel and entertainment, depends to a large degree upon discretionary income. If people feel insecure about their jobs, they spend less and save more. Though an increased savings rate can have a positive long-term effect on the economy, it tends to create short-term turmoil for retailers.

The retail grocery business is basic, and yet when times are tough, consolidation can take place, threatening job security somewhat. If you work for a food retailer, you can get a feeling for the health of the store by looking at the floor traffic. Is it busy? Also check to see whether the shelves are well stocked. If you see "back-filling"—placing the product on the outside edge of the shelf and leaving the back of the shelf empty—this could be a sign that the company is having cash-flow problems or operating losses.

Specialty stores for such things as sporting goods, gifts, and crafts can do well during challenging economic times if they address essential needs. If not, you will see specialty stores open and close continually, creating a difficult employment picture within that area. If your store is busy and well stocked, your job should be secure provided other subelements listed on the job security chart are positive.

The department store side of the retail industry is suffering the greatest. For example, in 1990 Campeau Corporation began its precipitous slide into bankruptcy. It operated 261 of the country's best-known department stores, generating $7.6 billion in annual sales. That amounted to more than 5 percent of total U.S. apparel sales. Campeau's demise was followed by numerous other Chapter 11 petitions and bankruptcies, causing a major shake-up in the retail industry. Many analysts feel the turmoil in department stores is a long way from over.

2. Region

As we have said before, the region in which you live greatly affects your potential job security. There are quantifiable economic elements that cause regions to prosper or pause. The three primary influences are: diversification, growth trends, and government stability. As we mentioned before, circle an item only if it is specifically relevant to your area.

Diversification refers to the assortment of businesses in your immediate area. Employment security is enhanced within a region if it has multiple business segments such as electronics, durable goods, and soft goods. Multiple business segments cushion the fluctuation caused by the changing prosperity of each segment. Domination of an area by coal, oil, or lumber production, for example, can adversely affect job security. If your region is *not* diversified, circle that item on the chart.

Are the majority of companies within your region affected by cycles and seasons? If so, employment will fluctuate unless the companies have countercycles. When a region has companies that counterbalance one another's cycles, job security is enhanced. If your region is dominated by cyclical businesses and they do not counterbalance one another, circle "Cyclical Businesses" on the chart.

Is your city dominated by one large employer, making it dependent upon the health of that company? Seattle spent many years watching its employment level ebb and flow with the health of The Boeing Company. Finally, during the 1980s, the region was able to diversify. It now has many companies representing a number of business segments, and the business cycles counterbalance one another. This makes Seattle a healthy employment region. If you work in Seattle, you would not circle any of the items under "Diversification."

Growth Trends' importance should be obvious. For the purpose of this chart, we are looking for signs of *negative* or *poor* growth. Today's business must be global in its view. Foreign competition affects every aspect of business. Even service businesses, which are people dependent, face competition from abroad. Domestic banking has encountered significant competition from foreign banks. Bank of America, for example, once the largest bank in the world, is now ranked fifteenth behind several European and Japanese banks. If your *region* is not actively engaged in international business, circle "Non-Global Focus."

A second subelement affecting a region's growth is its population. People make business. If people are leaving an area, jobs disappear because there are fewer people needing goods and services. Look at some of the cities with the lowest unemployment rates as of December 1990: Milwaukee at 3.6 percent; San Francisco at 3.7 percent; Seattle at 3.9 percent. Each of these cities is growing. If your area is decreasing in population, circle that subelement.

The growth of an area is also affected when the companies within the area are not expanding. If you cannot look around and point to a number of companies that are enlarging and adding people, the overall economy in your area could begin to slide. Ray Kroc, the founder of McDonald's, is credited with saying, "You're either green and growing or you're ripe and rotten." There is a great deal of truth to that statement. If an area stops growing, it will very soon begin to decay and show an increase in unemployment. Circle this item if you do not see growing companies in your area.

The government's stability and strength influence a region's health, and thus your potential job security. You can remember the economic impact New York City's financial woes had upon employment. When a region's government is sick, police protection is affected making people leave for safer areas. If you have poor police protection in your area, circle the appropriate item. Poor government generally makes poor schools, and people will leave to find better education for their children. If your schools rank in the bottom half of schools in your state, circle "Poor Educational System"; it has an impact on your job security.

A poorly run local government levies higher taxes, making business flee to lower-taxed areas. If your area shows up among the top ten states with the highest taxes, circle "High Tax Rate." Your employer may be considering relocating to another city or state with lower taxes. Oregon, for example, has a very high personal income tax rate. Just across the river is Washington, with *no* personal income tax. Every year, many companies move "across the river" to save on taxes for their employees.

Those of you living in major metropolitan areas may find that you are circling all three subelements in this category. What does that mean to you? Well, for one thing, the size of your area increases your chance of *finding* another job. But the obvious instability of the economy increases *turnover* in jobs.

Look around. Count the number of companies that open and close in a year. Add to that the number of companies that relocate outside of your city. You'll see that *big* (meaning "big city") helps with job security in terms of getting a job, but not necessarily in keeping the job.

3. Profession

The level of management at which you work greatly affects your job security. For the purpose of this chart, you will circle just one of the subelements under either "Management," "Staff," or "Line," provided a subelement applies to your job. Remember, greater job security is based upon the lowest score. If none of the subelements listed fits your job title or description, don't worry about it, be happy. It means your security as it relates to this factor is good. If several subelements apply to your position, find the one that describes the *dominant* aspect of your job. For example, you may do a small amount of customer service, such as answering the telephone, but your job is defined as accounting. In that case circle only "Accounting."

Executive managers, corporate vice presidents, and above are more vulnerable to layoffs than middle or frontline managers. They comprise a small percentage of the total number of unemployed, but that is because top management is such a small percentage of the total employment base. However, the experience of two recent client companies can illustrate how vulnerable top management is. One client employed 400 people, 6 of whom were top executives. In a recent cutback, 39 workers were laid off, representing roughly 10 percent of the force. However, the executive staff was cut to 4, a reduction of 33 percent. Another client had a staff of 125 people, including 4 executives. They reduced their staff by 15, a 12 percent reduction, but they also cut one executive, a 25 percent reduction. If you are a vice president or above, circle "Executive."

Corporations are trying to cut costs and improve their responsiveness to changing markets. One way to accomplish this is to reduce layers of management. Many companies have as many as twelve levels of management between frontline supervisors and the president of the company. New management philosophy says that a company cannot respond to market changes if there are more than six management layers. Most middle managers filter and analyze information; they do not sell, build, wrap, or ship the product. Reducing the number of middle managers means fewer people debating a decision, so decisions can be made more rapidly. Fewer middle managers also means less overhead. If you are neither a vice president nor a frontline manager, and you are in management, circle "Middle" on the chart.

It is frontline supervision that is most productive within the ranks of management. Frontline managers are often called supervisors. They are the first level of management within an organization. Very often frontline managers have productive tasks to perform in addition to supervisory issues and problems to resolve. Your security as a frontline manager should be adversely affected only if you supervise fewer than three people (the typical span of control is considered seven people), in which case someone may determine that your crew can be supervised by another manager, reducing overhead by one person. If you are a frontline supervisor as we have defined it, circle that item on the chart.

Staff positions are support functions. They are usually positions that process and analyze information. That is exactly what computers do, and computers have had an impact upon staff positions. For instance, in the 1960s and early 1970s a company with $100 million in annual sales could have employed forty or fifty people in its accounting department. Today that same company would need only twelve people and a computer.

Staff positions are always looked at first when a company is considering cost reductions. To determine the vulnerability of your job if you are staff, ask yourself how important you are to the overall functioning of the company, and whether your tasks can be done by a computer. If your importance is negligible or if a computer could do your job, you may not be as secure in your job as you might think otherwise. If your job definition or the department for which you work is accounting, administration, or marketing, circle the appropriate item on the chart.

Line personnel often have budget responsibility, or at the very least have a direct effect upon revenue or profit. Line positions are generally more secure than staff *unless* there are simply too many people doing the same job. The primary line positions targeted during a cutback are production, customer contact people, and sales representatives. An example of a position that could be cut is that of a salesperson who is not generating enough revenue. Most businesses with a direct sales force believe a territory must generate between $2 million and $5 million a year to pay the salesman's overhead and earn an acceptable profit. If you are a direct salesperson with a territory producing less than that, your job could be in jeopardy unless your product is far more profitable than average or your territory is growing rapidly. If your job or department is one of the three listed under the heading "Line," circle that item. If you did not find your job listed, count that as a good sign.

4. Company Size

The three most important subelements affecting your company are expansion, profits, and diversification (participation in diverse markets and multiple product areas). Their impact depends upon the size of the company. A small company usually cannot sustain itself very long if it fails to grow or expand. It will have to cut costs, and people are the first to go. A medium or large company will cut staff if there is no growth, but will not cut as fast as a small company. These differences are reflected in the weighted numbers on the chart under each respective heading. If you work for a company that isn't growing, circle that description on the chart under the appropriate company size heading.

Earlier we explained the relationship between profit and the size of a company when we discussed Ford Motor Company. Cash is king in today's business; companies need cash to operate. Cash is a by-product of profits, in the form of either actual cash flow or borrowing power. Small companies usually have little cash available, lessening their tolerance of difficult times. If "Poor Profitability" (1 percent or less) is a problem in your company, circle the appropriate item. If profits are good, be thankful.

Small companies are rarely diversified. Their prosperity is usually based upon finding and working a well-defined niche in their market, so lack of diversification does not have a great impact on job security. (You will note that the weighted number for "No Diversification" is lowest under "Small" for company size.) However, larger companies often depend upon diversification to weather business cycles. When one area is down, another will be up, stabilizing the company overall. Without diversification, layoffs will be used as a major tool to cut costs quickly in response to soft markets. Circle "No Diversification" under the appropriate heading if it applies to your company.

5. Education

A college degree is always an asset. However, a degree that is not in demand, such as home economics, English literature, or social studies, won't compete with an M.B.A. in most businesses. There are more people with advanced degrees in the job market than ever before. This makes a low-demand degree a somewhat negative asset. Add to that the lack of an advanced degree and your job security can be hurt. Chances are, if your company has a cutback you will compete with another person who has a high-demand degree—business, accounting, economics—and/or an advanced degree. To determine if your degree is low-demand in your industry, ask a human resources counselor to list the three most sought-after degrees when hiring. If your major is on that list, you have a high-demand degree for your industry.

The prestige of your school means little in keeping your job. It adds greatest value at the time of hiring, not firing. But if you had to compete with a graduate of a highly prestigious school during a layoff, it might make a difference if your school wasn't prestigious. So circle that item if applicable.

Trade or technical schooling costs you points if the field in which you trained is not in demand. Of course, if trade school has nothing to do with your training or education, ignore this category. If you were trained at a trade school, circle the appropriate subelements. Time within a field is important;

trade school training is usually short, and employers expect your actual on-the-job experience to make you a better employee. Ten years is generally considered the time required to become "senior" in one's skills and experience. As with college, a high-prestige trade school has little effect upon your job retention; its value is greatest at the time of hiring.

On-the-job training has value if the training is in demand and relevant to your actual job. Length of time is important because greater experience indicates greater capability. A successful track record within your field (e.g., letters of commendation, excellent performance appraisals) is very important. Too often in a layoff situation a person who learned on the job will be competing with someone who has either a college education or technical training. Without a strong track record he will lose. Circle elements under "On-the-Job Training" only if you *did not* train at a college or trade school, or if your formal training is not relevant to your current career.

Considering Independent Influences

At the bottom of the chart are four items labeled "Independent Factors." These have been included because they influence your job security, independent of the major factors we just discussed.

If you had the opportunity to sit in on a management meeting in which the topic of who's to stay and who's to go was being discussed, you might be surprised to learn how much executives and managers struggle with the issue. They try very hard to be fair and equitable. As a result, four factors often have an overriding influence upon their decision. The first factor is the strategic importance of a job. If your job is **critical** to the success of the company, you will be one of the last people out the door. For example, you may be working for a small electronics manufacturer that is losing money and is located in a depressed region. All of these subelements indicate poor job security. However, if your job is vital to the company, you will subtract five security points from your score because your job would be one of the last to go.

The second independent element is your performance

evaluation. If your evaluation has been **superior** or excellent, you will be eliminated after those who were rated less than superior.

The third independent element is **seniority.** If you are the most senior person within your department or skill group, your job will generally be eliminated last. "Most senior" is worth three security points.

The last independent influence is a question about previous layoffs. A study by *CFO* magazine indicated that companies that had used layoffs as a means of cutting costs were much more likely to use the method again. If within the past twelve months there has been a company layoff (usually defined as ten or more people being let go at the same time) and "cutting costs" was given as the reason for the action, add three points to your total score.

How to Compute Your Score

Circle every numbered subelement within the chart that relates to your job. (Remember, you may not find a subelement that relates specifically to your job under each category. That's okay.) Next, total these numbers. Then, if appropriate, add or subtract the independent influence points. Compare your score to the following rating system to determine how you stand:

Less than 30 points = Stable employment environment. You are in control of your timing. If you need a year to prepare for a change, you should have it—provided everything stays the same.

Between 31 and 60 points = Questionable employment stability. Pay close attention to the subelements rated 8, 9, or 10. Poor profitability and no growth, for example, may mean your company could lose its credit line, causing it to run out of operating cash. It could also be vulnerable to a takeover. Either event may mean an immediate loss of your job.

Your job- or career-change plans should include an effort to save "rainy day" money. Also, plan alternatives in the event you were to lose your job sooner than planned.

61 points or more = Poor job security. Perhaps there is some factor not mentioned on the chart that will help you keep your job longer than what is indicated; but all things considered, your job security is pretty shaky. You may want to set out on an immediate job search to find a more secure position. Once you have a job that guarantees a regular paycheck, you can then begin working on a long-term career plan. (As you will read in the next chapter, it is much easier to change jobs than to change careers. If you don't have the financial resources to bridge the change, your transition may require two steps. Initially, secure steady work; then do what it takes to make the long-term transition.) Don't panic, just be realistic about the situation. The score probably validated something you already knew.

If after you compute your score you feel something important is missing, do your best to factor it into your overall job security picture. Remember, the chart is only a guide—not the total answer—to how long you have to plan.

Using What You Have Learned

According to a *Newsweek* magazine poll, 74 percent of respondents could not afford to be out of work for more than one year. Today most middle management job changes take six months or more, and many take a year. If the individual actually wants to change *career fields*—remember 62 percent said they did—the total transition will undoubtedly take at least a year. That year does not have to be a year without work. If you plan well, the needed training, schooling, or preparation could be accomplished while you continue to work at your present job.

Now that you know how secure your job is, your career-change plan can be built around that knowledge. This brings you to the next step. You need to understand how your values have affected your decision making and job satisfaction. A mid-career change is filled with decisions. The next chapter offers you a method to follow that will help you work through the more difficult ones you face.

Compute Your Potential Job Security

	MANUFACTURING	*SERVICE*	*RETAIL*
INDUSTRY	5 Apparel 6 Electronics 10 Transportation	4 Medical 5 Travel/Entertainment 10 Financial	1 Food 3 Specialty 5 Department
REGION	*Diversification* 5 Limited Business Segments 5 Cyclical Businesses 7 One Dominant Company	*Growth Trends* 5 Non-Global Focus 4 Decreasing Population 7 Few Growing Companies	*Government Stability* 3 Poor Police System 5 Poor Educational System 7 High Tax Rate
PROFESSION	*Management* 5 Executive 3 Middle 1 Frontline Supervision	*Staff (Support)* 2 Accounting 3 Administration 4 Marketing	*Line (Budget Responsibility)* 1 Production 2 Customer Contact Person 3 Sales
COMPANY SIZE	*Small (<$50 million)* 9 No Expansion/Growth 10 Poor Profitability 4 No Diversification	*Medium ($50–$500 Million)* 8 No Expansion/Growth 8 Poor Profitability 5 No Diversification	*Large (>$500 Million)* 6 No Expansion/Growth 6 Poor Profitability 6 No Diversification

EDUCATION	College Degree	Trade/Technical Training	On-the-Job Training
	3 Low-Demand Major	3 Low-Demand Field	4 Low-Demand Field
	2 No Advanced Degree	4 $<$10 Years in Field	5 Limited Track Record
	1 Low-Prestige School	1 Low-Prestige School	5 $<$10 Years in Field

INDEPENDENT FACTORS:

- Subtract 5 points from your total if your job is critical to the success of the company.
- Subtract 3 points if your last performance evaluation was superior or above.
- Subtract 3 points if you are the most senior person within your department or skill area.
- Add 3 points if your company has had a downsizing layoff within the last 12 months.

HOW TO COMPUTE YOUR SCORE:

Circle each numbered item that relates to your job. Total these numbers. Add or subtract points for each independent influence item that relates to you. Compare your total to the scoring below.

SCORING: $<$ 30 points = Stable job; 31–60 points = Be careful; 61+ points = Little security.

Chapter 3

Personal Values and the Mid-Career Change

Do you know the single factor that has the most influence on job satisfaction? We will give you a hint. It is not money, or power, or prestige, or the fancy title on the door, or the brass nameplate on the desk. It is stress. Stress can make your job either heaven or hell.

There are two types of stress, constructive and destructive. Constructive stress can be one of the more enjoyable things about your job. Constructive stress results from business competition, the pursuit of goals, and the desire to achieve. This kind of stress can momentarily increase blood pressure and kick in adrenaline. This stress winds up a salesman for a crackerjack presentation or gives an extra boost to a ball player who must hit in the tie-breaking run.

Destructive stress may be the reason you want to make a mid-career change. When a friend tells you he left his job because "the pressure" got to him, this is destructive stress. It results in depression, high blood pressure, ulcers, heart attack, and a vulnerable immune system. Too much destructive stress can kill you. It can also be murder on family relationships.

In most instances, the cause of destructive stress is a **values conflict.** Your personal values and those demanded from you by your career are not the same. You may be aware of the problem; or it may be so subtle that you only know you are unhappy and feel discontent at work, but don't know why. Values can provide career guidance when you understand them. They are critical for two reasons: 1) You never take any action without making a decision, and you never make a decision without consulting your values at your conscious or subconscious level. 2) As previously mentioned, destructive stress often results in career dissatisfaction. Its cause is a values conflict. You cannot resolve a conflict until you understand the *nature* of the conflict.

An example of someone with a values conflict is Joe, a sales representative for Midwestern Office Products. Joe has been an office products salesman for fifteen years, the last five with MOP. He was starting his sixth year when MOP was sold. The new owner told everyone that the company would keep up its reputation for outstanding value and products, but that is not what happened. To support the huge debt acquired in buying the company, the new owner began replacing many of the product lines with cheaper ones. He also decreased the size of the customer service department to save money on overhead. Joe noticed discrepancies in purchase-order fulfillment. Inferior goods were being substituted for the ordered product. His customers began to complain about quality and service.

Joe approached his new boss and explained the problem. Instead of finding a sympathetic ear, he was told that this was the new order of business and if he did not like it he could find a job elsewhere.

A tight economy and good pay made Joe feel he had no choice but to stay. At his annual physical examination, Joe complained of chronic headaches. His doctor found that Joe's cholesterol and blood pressure were up. The doctor said these symptoms were the result of stress.

Joe's stress was not caused by a need to increase his performance; he was achieving his sales quota. Joe's values of honesty, quality, and service were in conflict with the values his
job demanded: compromising quality and service to maximize
profits.

Many people arrive at mid-career and realize that their job
demands a sacrifice of their personal values. Sometimes the
compromise is small enough to be tolerated. Other times it
causes enough destructive stress to lead to a mid-career
change.

Understanding Values

Frequently, people who divorce and remarry keep the same
problems, they just change the person involved. Mid-career
changers can fall into the same trap when their job or career
conflicts with their deeper personal values. Changing jobs will
not solve the problem until they resolve the values conflict.

Values can be understood best by picturing yourself as a
simple schematic (see page 45). Earlier we said that every
decision you make is based upon your values. You make
decisions with your brain, but your brain uses data; and in the
case of values, it gathers the data from three levels. In this
illustration, the levels are represented by the skin, gut, and
heart. The skin is the **reactive** level, which is influenced by
circumstances and your daily environment. The gut is the **gut**
level, where you store your conditioned responses and your
learned social behaviors. The heart is the **core** level, where
your innate and universal values are found.

Reactive

Like skin, reactive values respond to the immediate environment. If you are in a benevolent environment, it's a good day,
and things are going well, your decisions/reactions will be
positive. If the environment becomes malevolent or threatening, your reactions will be self-centered and self-protecting,
regardless of the cost to others.

As a mid-career changer, you are concerned with the reac-

VALUES LEVELS

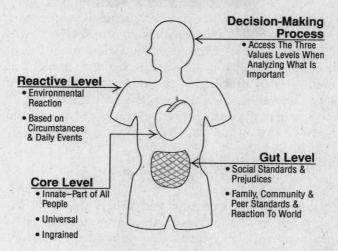

Decision-Making Process
• Access The Three Values Levels When Analyzing What Is Important

Reactive Level
• Environmental Reaction
• Based on Circumstances & Daily Events

Core Level
• Innate—Part of All People
• Universal
• Ingrained

Gut Level
• Social Standards & Prejudices
• Family, Community & Peer Standards & Reaction To World

tive level because you don't want to make shortsighted, self-centered decisions that you later will regret. The stress and pressure you are feeling at this point in your life make you vulnerable to the reactive level. You need to be able to look beyond the moment and keep in touch with your other values. A reactive values response would be to tell your boss to "take this job and shove it." That might feel good at the time, but within twenty-four hours you would regret the decision.

Gut

Values at this level are the result of childhood experiences with your parents, family, teachers, and friends. You learn values by watching what people do rather than listening to what they say. Your childhood associations are particularly influential between the ages of ten and twenty.

Gut values are very powerful values; they influence every major decision you make. They form your views about what is important to you and yours. They define what you accept as right and wrong. Your social standards and personal preju-dices are held at this level. Because they are learned at a young age, often from a small group of people, gut values tend to be narrow and self-protective. These ingrained gut-level values rarely change as you get older. How self-centered your gut-level values are is influenced by how attuned you are to your core values. Troubled relationships at work or at home, or a mid-career crisis that seems insurmountable may mean that you are operating from a self-centered gut level. You are focusing on your problems and your concerns; you are not giving consideration to other people's needs. Reach down to the very center of your being, to your core, and access the unselfish values you find there.

Core

Core values are the principles and beliefs that you actually want to guide your life. Core values are we-centered rather than self-centered. They are ancient values that have stood the test of centuries. These values are the heart of all major religions, cultures, and philosophical systems found throughout the world. They are innate values that have promoted human survival. These are your deepest values. They can best be defined by listing nine universal core values:

1. The world is an open opportunity; people choose to make life a heaven or a hell.
2. People are basically good; they would rather help than hurt others.
3. People make responsible choices; when given a chance, they learn and grow.
4. The ends are justified only if the means are honorable.
5. Do unto others as you would have them do unto you.
6. All people deserve the right to choose their path, so long as others are not harmed. Likewise, they even deserve the right to fail and make mistakes.
7. The true worth of people is in their contributions to the world, rather than their appearance, their race, their religion, or their socioeconomic status.
8. As you sow, so shall you reap.
9. Each of us owes something to this world; we want to leave the world a better place.

The more in touch you are with these values, the more optimistic you feel and the easier life can be. Long-term success and good personal and professional relationships are more easily maintained when your actions are consistent with your core values.

Deciphering the Conflict

Joe's values conflict was between his **gut**-level behaviors required to perform his job, and his **core** principles and beliefs of what is right. This conflict causes almost all mid-career burnout.

Think how often you have heard someone say, "It's not *what* you know, it's *who* you know that counts around here." Or they say, "To survive around here you'd better do unto others *before* they do unto you." What is being described by such talk is a work environment—gut-level social standards—that conflict with your core principles and beliefs.

When you were young, you rationalized the behavior. After all, in high school the super athletes always got passing grades whether or not they studied. Your gut level accepted this behavior because of conditioning.

As you mature, what is important to you begins to change. It is less important to be accepted by everyone and more important to like yourself. In other words, your values emphasis begins to shift. Whether you realize it or not, you begin to want your behavior and your surroundings to be more consistent with your core values.

You could react like the character Dudley Moore plays in the movie *Crazy People*. One day you simply say you can't lie about the products anymore. You want to tell the truth. Or you respond as a malpractice lawyer once did. You decide that representing fakes isn't worth the millions of dollars in fees you have earned. You decide you want to be honest, you want to be *you*.

If you are feeling stress on the job, you probably have a conflict between the social standards required for success and the principles you believe should earn success.

If you try to resolve the conflict by simply changing jobs,

and you don't take the time to decipher the cause of the conflict, you are almost guaranteed to take the problems with you. You'll change the setting, not the conflict, and you will still suffer from stress and depression, the primary symptoms of mid-career syndrome.

Matching Values to Your Career

Joe's problem is all too common in today's business world. Poor economic conditions and dog-eat-dog competition make many businesses operate too aggressively. We have two aids that can help you make your mid-career change result in an environment compatible with your personal values.

First, look at the Values Conflict chart that follows. Identify the gut behaviors you experience and note the core principles with which they are in conflict. List any other values that relate specifically to your job.

Next develop a list of questions you can ask prospective employers. (Use the examples indicated on the Values Conflict chart.) Your list should have questions pinpointing principles and standards that you personally want in your work, and they should help you spot what you want to avoid. When you go out on job interviews, ask these questions so you can understand the values of the prospective employer and minimize the chance of future conflicts.

Being in mid-career means you are undoubtedly a very busy person balancing career and family responsibilities. It has probably been a long time since you sat down in a quiet corner and took stock of your personal values. You need to take the time to do so.

Once you are familiar with your own values, you can analyze the type of stress you are under in your present position. Understanding your values can turn your current career crisis into a rewarding (and lasting) career change.

In these first three chapters we have:

- defined mid-career syndrome;
- assessed your job security; and
- examined the relationship between values and stress.

Values Conflict

Gut Reactions & Standards	*Core Principles & Beliefs*
1. Do unto others *before* they do unto you.	1. Do unto others *as* you would that they do unto you.
2. It's *who* you know that counts.	2. It's *what* you know that counts.
3. Whitewash what you say to make it sound good.	3. Tell the truth.
4. People are mushrooms, fed ——— and kept in the dark.	4. People should know the facts and have open communication.
5. It's your style that counts.	5. It's your contribution that counts.
6. Profits before quality.	6. Quality ensures profits.

Sample Interview Questions

1. What kind of conflicts seem to arise between people, and how do you resolve them?
2. What earns a person a promotion?
3. Is the communication style here direct and straightforward? How important is it to be politically sensitive?
4. How open is management with problems and business plans?
5. What is the most valued characteristic in an employee?
6. Rank the real operating relationships between quality, profits, and customer service.

Now you are ready to start the tactical process of building your career plan. This begins with defining the kind of change you want to make.

Chapter 4

You Have Skills That Will Travel

IN ORDER TO DETERMINE the kind of mid-career change you want to make, you need to understand the available options. This chapter has three objectives: first, to help you quantify your knowledge and skills; second, to show you how to transfer these assets into another career field and retain your *career equity* (the dollar value of your knowledge and skills); and third, to identify your dominant personality style and use it as a guide for career transition. (At the end of this chapter you will find forty Career Profile charts, which note the major skills required for success in each field.)

Quantifying Your Knowledge and Skills

Most people making a mid-career change understand more than they realize. They gain knowledge or skills in one situation but fail to see the various other areas to which that same knowledge or those same skills apply. It's a terrible mistake. So much of your knowledge of processes, production, people management, time management, and so on can transfer from one career to another.

To maximize your career-change opportunities, you need to discover your hidden knowledge. You have to find knowledge and skills that can transfer into new areas, allowing you to become an expert rapidly. For years you have been learning and gaining skills. You have, of course, learned specialized professional skills, but you have also gained knowledge and skills from other areas of your life. Many of these have value in your career.

Catching "Nonprofessional" Skills with Professional Value

Being a Little League baseball coach is an example of an outside interest that develops professional skills. Every technique you use to motivate the kids and manage their parents can be applied in the work environment. In order to build a championship team, you have to motivate underachievers, deal with egos, manage personality conflicts, schedule practices, and arrange transportation. You also have to carefully negotiate differences between players, and diplomatically solve disputes among parents. These are practical management skills. As a successful team coach, you have learned leadership skills that are priceless in the working world.

Human resources managers feel that time management is one of the most important skills needed in a management candidate. If you have been working at a job with set tasks, you may not realize your skill in this area. You may have to look outside your workplace to assess your time management ability. How many outside activities do you have? Do you belong to several clubs? Do you do community work? Do you carry responsibilities at church? Do you manage your home and also work a full-time job? If you answered yes to any of these questions, then you possess time management skills.

Don't sell yourself short. We all learn from what we already know. List the after-work activities in which you participate. Do your best to note the managerial skills and knowledge you have gained from these activities, as we demonstrated in the Little League coach example. (Please note: many times you use managerial skills even when you are not a "manager." For example, you could be responsible for the successful completion of a set of tasks that involve the help of three other people. These people don't report to you, but you have to help them organize, prioritize, and process the information you need to complete your tasks. You are using managerial skills.) Use the Career Skills Evaluation chart on page 64 as a guide to help you identify skills that you use. It lists twenty-four of the most important transferable management skills. Make a real effort to be thorough in this exercise; the assessment will be invaluable if you decide to change career fields.

Quantifying Your Work Skills

The next step in your program is to *quantify* the skills you use in your actual job. It is often difficult for people to be objective when evaluating their own strengths, weaknesses, talents, and skills. You may want to enlist the help of others.

The Career Skills Evaluation chart is your tool for this exercise. Make a dozen copies of the chart. Evaluate your skills in the designated areas. Be as honest and objective as possible. You should not flatter yourself. You need unbiased information. Think of yourself as your boss filling out your annual performance review, or as a manager looking to hire you.

Use the following rating system:

1 = Demonstrated use of the skill on a few occasions
2 = Demonstrated use of the skill on numerous occasions
3 = Demonstrated use of the skill with consistent success
4 = Exceptional use of the skill
5 = Top performer in use of the skill

After completing your self-evaluation, ask several friends (seven is ideal) to evaluate your skills using the same criteria. The more input you can get at this time, the more accurate your evaluation will be. This rating process is in many respects the heart of the career-change process: you need its results to evaluate the strengths of your transferable skills, to determine your earning potential, and to construct your resume. Get others' perspectives if at all possible.

Following is a definition of each skill area listed on the chart. Study these definitions before you fill out the chart, and give them to anyone you ask to do an evaluation.

Administrative: Managing or directing the execution, application, or conduct of systems comprising more than one activity or group or person.

Delegation: Not doing the work yourself but letting or assigning other people (e.g., subordinate employees) to do it, the results of which are your responsibility.

Financial: Knowing about debits, credits, and running the financial side of a business.

Leadership: Inspiring others to pursue a common vision, accomplish a given task, or achieve a common goal.

Marketing: Knowing how and why people buy products and services.

Motivation: Inducing people to do what you want done, not by the authority to command action, but by creating incentives for people to act from their own desire.

Production: Knowing the general methods, equipment, and processes required to manufacture or mass-produce a product.

Project Management: Directing, controlling, or planning a series of activities with a specified outcome and deadline.

Time Management: Using time efficiently when it is a significant part of the success of an activity.

Training Others: Teaching subject matter or job processes by explaining, demonstrating, and then supervising practice; this does not include routine on-the-job coaching, but rather the planning of an organized training activity and the application of training methods.

Listening: Remaining attentive to people speaking, then understanding and remembering what they say.

Negotiation: Exchanging ideas, information, and opinions with others, and arriving jointly at decisions, conclusions, or solutions.

Persuasion: Influencing others in favor of your product, service, course of action, or point of view.

Public Speaking: Standing with poise before a group of people to make a formal presentation.

Verbal Clarity: Expressing yourself by speaking fluently and with conviction, so that people easily understand and remember what you say.

Written Clarity: Expressing yourself in writing with conciseness, good organization, proper sentence structure, and vocabulary suited to the reader, so that they easily understand and remember what you write.

Computer Application: Knowing 1) business-related computer hardware and software, 2) how to use computer technology to accomplish work, and 3) how to adapt computer technology to a work setting.

Computer Expertise: Knowing how to program computers and use all or almost all hardware-based functions.

Advanced Degree: A college degree requiring education beyond a four-year bachelor's degree; for example, master's degree, Ph.D., or Ed.D. For this item, measure the importance of the degree as it relates to your chosen career field and the prestige of the school from which it was obtained.

Technical School: Vocational training—as opposed to academic training—to prepare for a certain job or class of jobs; emphasis is on short-term training to acquire job skills typically offered by two-year community colleges or private trade schools. Measure the value of the training by how well it has prepared you for future career opportunities.

OJT (on-the-job training): Learning a job from a qualified worker or trainer while performing the tasks. Rate this item based upon the transferability of the knowledge. Sometimes OJT relates too specifically to one organization's way of doing business.

Positive: A disposition or tendency to look on the more favorable side of events and to anticipate the most favorable result; seeing problems as opportunities.

Outgoing: Enjoying interaction with people; good at mixing with and meeting new people; people-oriented as opposed to object- and process-oriented.

Tenacious: Staying with an activity until it is finished, despite setbacks or slowed progress; willing to keep trying or even start over; not easily distracted or discouraged; willing to make every effort to succeed.

Tabulating Your Score

If you have been able to get ratings from others, you need to calculate an average for each item. Take a blank copy of the evaluation chart and total the scores for each rated item. Divide the sum by the number of people who evaluated you (including yourself), and the quotient is your average score. For example, let's say that for the item "Leadership" you received three ratings of 3 and four ratings of 4. This represents seven evaluations in total. The total score for that item is 25, the average score 3.57. Rounded off, this represents a rating of 4 for the skill "Leadership." As you will see in the forty Career Skills Evaluation charts found at the end of this chapter, a "Leadership" rating of 4 means that you have the skill proficiency required to meet the need of any career where leadership is rated "Essential."

Tabulate your average score for every item on the Career Skills Evaluation chart. You will use these scores to compare your skills against the skill requirements for the forty careers listed at the end of the chapter. This sheet will also be the basis for calculating your earning potential in Chapter 6. The directions for that calculation can be found on page 116.

Your final Career Skills Evaluation chart represents the **transferable** skills you have gathered up to this point in your career. The skills are transferable because each basic skill applies to any managerial job in any industry. A very specific example is found in Chapter 11: there we walk you through Steve Kelly's process of transferring his manufacturing managerial skills to a new position as video production manager for a cable television company. Though the jobs seem to be very different on the surface, once the tasks behind each skill are identified and described, it becomes evident that the requirements are *very* similar and the skills are *very* transferable.

How to Retain Career Equity

Not everyone reading this book will face the challenge of changing careers. As you will see in Chapter 5, some people deal with mid-career syndrome by changing jobs within their existing company or changing jobs within their existing industry. Both of these changes happen fairly easily and do not threaten senior career equity. Prospective employers assume a senior person with company or industry knowledge should be paid a senior wage. However, when choosing to leave a company or industry, many others *will* deal with the very real problem of **threatened career equity.** These people need to know how to make the change *and* retain their senior value.

Now you have taken stock of your assets. You have seen that you may have professionally valuable knowledge that's been labeled "personal" in the past; in Chapter 6 you will quantify—actually place a value upon—your transferable management skills. But next we want to help you see how you can change careers and *prove* that your skills are transferable to a new field and still worth their senior value.

People in mid-career often think that because they have been in one line of work or one industry for fifteen to twenty years they are locked in there. They fail to realize that most management jobs require the same skills. For example, a sales manager and a production manager both need to motivate, lead, control, and monitor people's activities. One manages the sales production, the other the manufacturing production. Each manager's respective knowledge of sales and manufacturing is important, but their management skills are of **greatest value.** An accountant in a retail firm has nearly the same responsibilities as an accountant in a manufacturing firm. Each may be keeping track of different information, but they both need the same quantitative ability and attention to detail. Both jobs have the same objective, keeping track of the income and outflow of money.

There are two steps you must take to prove to a prospective employer that your skills can transfer to a new industry or career and retain their value. First, you must research the prospective position and industry, ferreting out the similarities and differences. Second, you must learn how to show an employer that you can handle any situation you will encounter in the new industry.

Researching an Industry

In Chapter 10 we talk about networking to build prospective job opportunities. Here we want to talk about networking for another reason. We want to show you how to network a prospective career field so as to learn everything you can about it.

Every industry, and each company within it, thinks it is unique. This is just not so. We know your skills are transferable, but you have to prove it to an employer. You have to become an expert about the industry and then demonstrate your skills by using the industry's terms.

The best way to become an industry expert is to join a local chapter of the industry's trade association. Nearly every industry, from home building to elderly care-giving, has a trade association. Look in the telephone book and you will probably find the phone number listed. If not, talk to your local librarian; there are several books listing trade associations, such as *Encyclopedia of Associations*. These books often list when and where a trade association holds its annual or semiannual conferences. If you are really serious about a change, you should attend a national conference.

As you interact with the trade association, you will become familiar with the industry's jargon. You will learn, for example, that an accountant thinks of a customer as a "client," or that a credit union worker thinks of a customer as a "member." You know that whether customers are clients or members, your motivational management skills that energize superior customer service are transferable. As you talk to a credit union president, interviewing for a management job, you can tell a story noting how important "members" are and how you motivated a group of employees, turning a poor service problem into a superior service situation. By telling this story, using a situation he understands and jargon he uses, your senior career equity will retain its value in his eyes. He will believe that you understand his business.

Proving Your Skills Can Transfer

Trade associations know what problems face their industry. Their training programs address the pressing issues and teach problem-solving techniques. After attending a program, take these techniques and review your experience for situations similar to the problems being demonstrated. Then relate your situation to your target industry using its jargon. Voilà, you have transcended the abyss that kept you in one industry. Use this process with every industry problem you identify. Soon you will learn what is unique about the industry, and more important, you will see how similar its problems are to those of other industries.

When you secure an interview, your greatest task is to prove that you can move your knowledge across industries without losing any effectiveness. Using an industry's jargon during the interview proves you are familiar with its problems. Telling stories that demonstrate how you solved similar problems secures your position as an expert.

You must learn how to tell good stories. They don't have to be long, but they must be real and believable. When you attend industry meetings, listen for specific problems. Then search your experience and find a similar situation. *Write down* some of the details of your problem situation and its solution. Make sure you fully understand how the solution was developed. Translate the story into the industry's jargon, and practice telling it. Keeping notes will help you remember it. Tell the story to several friends and ask them how clear and logical it is. During an interview find an opportunity to interject one or two of these industry-tailored stories.

David is someone who changed industries and used several stories to demonstrate his knowledge. He was a credit manager for a large retail business specializing in men's clothing. He loved working with computers and he wanted very much to work in the computer business. Since he'd had a career in the clothing business for thirteen years, his friends advised him not to try to change industries. But by attending an industry conference, David discovered that the computer business and the clothing business use the same distribution channels and have many of the same customers. Both sell a portion of their product line directly to major retailers such as Sears and Montgomery Ward.

When David interviewed for the credit manager's job with a computer company, he was able to tell two carefully rehearsed stories about collection problems with major retailers, thereby demonstrating his skill and showing how well he understood the challenges faced by the computer business. These stories, along with his other knowledge of the industry, proved he could transfer into the new industry as an expert and retain his senior career equity. Today David is the credit manager for a major computer manufacturer. He loves working with a "leading edge" company. He was able to make the change because he was willing to invest the time, effort, and dollars required to make a successful career transition.

Discovering How Many Careers Use Your Skills

Now that you recognize your knowledge and skills, and know how to transfer them to new careers and industries, it is time to get a feeling for the variety of careers available. The Career Profile charts in this chapter represent career options in forty fields. They are in alphabetical order by career title. The management skills you quantified earlier are ranked on each chart as either "Nonessential," "Useful," or "Essential." Browse through the collection, matching your quantified skills with the needs of each career field. Use the following conversion guide to compare your own scores with these career fields.

- A rating of 4 or 5 on your chart equals an "Essential" rating on a Career Profile chart.
- A rating of 3 on your chart equals a "Useful" rating on a Career Profile chart.
- Any rating under 3 means your proficiency is inadequate for a skill rated "Useful" or "Essential."

The argument could be made that one needs almost every skill listed to succeed at any of these careers we have evaluated. However, for our purposes, we have pared down each job to its bare essentials. Each skill's value is based upon how *essential* it is to the performance of the respective job. For example, take the "Communication" skill group and the occupations of banker and biologist. Today bankers do a great deal of selling; thus the communication skills of listening, negotiating, and verbal and written clarity are essential for success. By contrast, biologists are researchers. Although they must be good at listening to other experts within their field, and capable of writing clearly about their research results, negotiation, persuasion, and verbal clarity are not *essential* skills for success.

Matching Your Personality and Your Career Choice

At the top of the Career Profile charts you will find a Career Personality Profile Group. Each career has been matched to the most suitable dominant personality type. Matching natural personality traits to career demands will reduce one source of gut-level values conflict.

A brief explanation of each personality type follows:

Analytical. A person who needs something tangible in every situation. Someone who looks for the pluses and minuses and wants every peg to fit in its slot.

Director. A person who wants to control every situation. Someone who likes being a leader and is willing to take the responsibility.

Supporter. A person who wants to feel comfortable in every situation. Someone who wants to belong and wants everyone to be a friend.

Entertainer. A person who needs recognition. Someone who likes to make things happen; they want action.

If you are familiar with these personality types and know where you fit, look at the jobs grouped under that classification. If you have never taken a personality test and do not have any idea which type best describes you, here is a simple test to help you find out.

Personality Style Test

Read the descriptions under each group. Circle the words that best describe you *at work*.

GROUP A
- Analytical, logical
- Considers all sides of an issue
- Would prefer to let things happen
- Prefers rules, procedures, systems
- Suspicious of people who rely on feelings
- Listener
- Patient
- Prefers to delay making decisions
- A rational thinker
- Good with technical issues

GROUP B
- Driving
- Competitive
- Leader
- Uncompromising
- Likes to get a general impression
- Wants a decision one way or the other
- Self-reliant
- Quick decision maker
- Controls emotions
- Likes orderly environment

GROUP C
- Amiable
- Supportive
- Pleasant
- Softhearted
- Uncomfortable with theories
- Inner-world oriented/ introspective
- Deliberate
- Wants to be comfortable
- Likes to keep a low profile
- Likes to help others

GROUP D
- Optimistic
- Animated
- Impatient
- Good talker
- Persuasive
- Passionate
- Likes concepts, ideas, theories
- Flashy
- Likes to have a high profile
- Relates well to people

Evaluating the Test

To determine your dominant personality style, count the items that you circled under each group. The group under which you have the greatest number of items circled is probably your dominant personality type. If you circled a relatively equal number of words under more than one group, you have learned to manage yourself for a more balanced personality. This is neither good nor bad. Everyone has a dominant style, yet many of us have learned to adapt to varied situations. Read the group descriptions again and see which is most like you.

Group A represents Analytical.

Group B represents Director.

Group C represents Supporter.

Group D represents Entertainer.

For your convenience, the following lists sort the careers into their respective personality groups.

ANALYTICAL:

Accountant/
  Bookkeeper
Banker
Biologist
Civil Engineer
Computer
  Programmer/Analyst
Drafter
Economist
Electronics Engineer
Forester/
  Conservationist
Industrial Engineer
Market Researcher
Underwriter

DIRECTOR:

Architect
City/County Manager
CPA—Manager/Partner
Doctor/Dentist
Entrepreneur
Health Services
  Manager
Labor Relations
  Specialist
Lawyer
Long-haul Truck
  Driver/Owner
Police Officer
Reporter/Journalist
Retail Owner/Manager

SUPPORTER:
Counselor
Librarian
Nurse
Occupational Therapist
Personnel Specialist
Psychologist
Radiology Technologist
Social Worker
Teacher/Professor

ENTERTAINER:
Clothing Designer
Graphic Artist
Hotel Manager
Public Relations
Specialist
Salesperson
Stockbroker
Travel Agent

Getting It All Together

There is an important goal we are trying to accomplish with the use of your skills evaluation, your personality assessment, and the Career Profiles we have prepared for your perusal. *We want to expand your horizons.* We want you to realize your potential and to discover the possibilities that are out there. The exercise you just went through is not a complicated, validated psychological test. Although it has been conducted on thousands of individuals with consistent results, it has not been validated under strict scientific conditions. We cannot give you a "confidence rating" regarding its scientific accuracy. Rather, through your growing self-knowledge and increased self-awareness, we want you to become more informed about career possibilities.

This chapter should have helped you recognize the transferability of your skills and knowledge. During this time of transition, it is wise to consider a new career even if you have not worked in that field before. If your personality and your skills match with a career field that has held some interest for you in the past, give yourself the chance to at least find out more about it.

By now, you know that most of your skills can transfer to a new career field, and you know how to prove to an employer the value of those skills. The next step is to learn how much effort is required in making various job/career changes.

Career Skills Evaluation Chart

Skill Scoring: (Check)   *Limited Performance* to *Top Performance*

MANAGEMENT:	1	2	3	4	5
Administrative	___	___	___	___	___
Delegation	___	___	___	___	___
Financial	___	___	___	___	___
Leadership	___	___	___	___	___
Marketing	___	___	___	___	___
Motivation	___	___	___	___	___
Production	___	___	___	___	___
Project Management	___	___	___	___	___
Time Management	___	___	___	___	___
Training Others	___	___	___	___	___
COMMUNICATION:					
Listening	___	___	___	___	___
Negotiation	___	___	___	___	___
Persuasion	___	___	___	___	___
Public Speaking	___	___	___	___	___
Verbal Clarity	___	___	___	___	___
Written Clarity	___	___	___	___	___
COMPUTER SKILLS:					
Application	___	___	___	___	___
Expertise	___	___	___	___	___
SPECIALIZED SKILLS:					
Advanced Degree	___	___	___	___	___
Technical School	___	___	___	___	___
OJT	___	___	___	___	___
ATTITUDINAL:					
Positive	___	___	___	___	___
Outgoing	___	___	___	___	___
Tenacious	___	___	___	___	___

Career Profile

Career Personality Profile Group: ANALYTICAL
Occupation: Accountant/Bookkeeper

Skill Scoring: (Check)	Non-essential	Useful	Essential
MANAGEMENT:	0, 1, 2	3	4, 5
Administrative			×
Delegation		×	
Financial			×
Leadership		×	
Marketing	×		
Motivation	×		
Production	×		
Project Management		×	
Time Management			×
Training Others		×	
COMMUNICATION:			
Listening			×
Negotiation		×	
Persuasion		×	
Public Speaking		×	
Verbal Clarity		×	
Written Clarity			×
COMPUTER SKILLS:			
Application			×
Expertise	×		
SPECIALIZED SKILLS:			
Advanced Degree		×	
Technical School			×
OJT		×	
ATTITUDINAL:			
Positive	×		
Outgoing	×		
Tenacious			×

Career Profile

Career Personality Profile Group: DIRECTOR
Occupation: <u>Architect</u>

Skill Scoring: (Check)	Non-essential	Useful	Essential
MANAGEMENT:	0, 1, 2	3	4, 5
Administrative	___	×	___
Delegation	___	×	___
Financial	___	×	___
Leadership	___	×	___
Marketing	___	___	×
Motivation	___	___	×
Production	×	___	___
Project Management	___	___	×
Time Management	___	___	×
Training Others	___	×	___
COMMUNICATION:			
Listening	___	___	×
Negotiation	___	___	×
Persuasion	___	___	×
Public Speaking	___	×	___
Verbal Clarity	___	___	×
Written Clarity	___	___	×
COMPUTER SKILLS:			
Application	___	___	×
Expertise	×	___	___
SPECIALIZED SKILLS:			
Advanced Degree	___	×	___
Technical School	___	___	×
OJT	___	×	___
ATTITUDINAL:			
Positive	___	×	___
Outgoing	___	×	___
Tenacious	___	___	×

Career Profile

Career Personality Profile Group: ANALYTICAL
Occupation: <u>Banker</u>

Skill Scoring: (Check)	*Non-essential*	*Useful*	*Essential*
MANAGEMENT:	0, 1, 2	3	4, 5
Administrative	—	—	×
Delegation	—	×	—
Financial	—	—	×
Leadership	—	×	—
Marketing	—	×	—
Motivation	—	×	—
Production	×	—	—
Project Management	—	×	—
Time Management	—	×	—
Training Others	—	×	—
COMMUNICATION:			
Listening	—	—	×
Negotiation	—	—	×
Persuasion	—	—	×
Public Speaking	—	×	—
Verbal Clarity	—	—	×
Written Clarity	—	—	×
COMPUTER SKILLS:			
Application	—	—	×
Expertise	×	—	—
SPECIALIZED SKILLS:			
Advanced Degree	×	—	—
Technical School	×	—	—
OJT	—	×	—
ATTITUDINAL:			
Positive	×	—	—
Outgoing	—	×	—
Tenacious	—	×	—

Career Profile

Career Personality Profile Group: ANALYTICAL
Occupation: Biologist

Skill Scoring: (Check)	Non-essential	Useful	Essential
MANAGEMENT:	0, 1, 2	3	4, 5
Administrative		✕	
Delegation	✕		
Financial	✕		
Leadership	✕		
Marketing	✕		
Motivation		✕	
Production	✕		
Project Management	✕		
Time Management			✕
Training Others		✕	
COMMUNICATION:			
Listening			✕
Negotiation	✕		
Persuasion		✕	
Public Speaking		✕	
Verbal Clarity		✕	
Written Clarity			✕
COMPUTER SKILLS:			
Application		✕	
Expertise	✕		
SPECIALIZED SKILLS:			
Advanced Degree		✕	
Technical School	✕		
OJT		✕	
ATTITUDINAL:			
Positive	✕		
Outgoing	✕		
Tenacious			✕

Career Profile

Career Personality Profile Group: DIRECTOR
Occupation: City/County Manager

Skill Scoring: (Check)	Non-essential	Useful	Essential
MANAGEMENT:	0, 1, 2	3	4, 5
Administrative			×
Delegation			×
Financial			×
Leadership			×
Marketing			×
Motivation			×
Production	×		
Project Management		×	
Time Management			×
Training Others		×	
COMMUNICATION:			
Listening			×
Negotiation			×
Persuasion			×
Public Speaking			×
Verbal Clarity			×
Written Clarity		×	
COMPUTER SKILLS:			
Application		×	
Expertise	×		
SPECIALIZED SKILLS:			
Advanced Degree	×		
Technical School	×		
OJT		×	
ATTITUDINAL:			
Positive			×
Outgoing			×
Tenacious			×

Career Profile

Career Personality Profile Group: ANALYTICAL
Occupation: Civil Engineer

Skill Scoring: (Check)	Non-essential	Useful	Essential
MANAGEMENT:	0, 1, 2	3	4, 5
Administrative		×	
Delegation	×		
Financial	×		
Leadership		×	
Marketing	×		
Motivation	×		
Production	×		
Project Management			×
Time Management		×	
Training Others	×		
COMMUNICATION:			
Listening			×
Negotiation	×		
Persuasion		×	
Public Speaking		×	
Verbal Clarity		×	
Written Clarity		×	
COMPUTER SKILLS:			
Application			×
Expertise		×	
SPECIALIZED SKILLS:			
Advanced Degree		×	
Technical School			×
OJT		×	
ATTITUDINAL:			
Positive		×	
Outgoing	×		
Tenacious			×

Career Profile

Career Personality Profile Group: ENTERTAINER
Occupation: <u>Clothing Designer</u>

Skill Scoring: (Check)	Non-essential	Useful	Essential
MANAGEMENT:	0, 1, 2	3	4, 5
Administrative		×	
Delegation	×		
Financial	×		
Leadership		×	
Marketing			×
Motivation		×	
Production		×	
Project Management		×	
Time Management		×	
Training Others		×	
COMMUNICATION:			
Listening			×
Negotiation			×
Persuasion			×
Public Speaking			×
Verbal Clarity			×
Written Clarity		×	
COMPUTER SKILLS:			
Application		×	
Expertise	×		
SPECIALIZED SKILLS:			
Advanced Degree	×		
Technical School		×	
OJT		×	
ATTITUDINAL:			
Positive		×	
Outgoing			×
Tenacious			×

Career Profile

Career Personality Profile Group: ANALYTICAL
Occupation: Computer Programmer/Analyst

Skill Scoring: (Check)	Non-essential	Useful	Essential
MANAGEMENT:	0, 1, 2	3	4, 5
Administrative			×
Delegation		×	
Financial		×	
Leadership		×	
Marketing	×		
Motivation		×	
Production	×		
Project Management			×
Time Management			×
Training Others		×	
COMMUNICATION:			
Listening			×
Negotiation		×	
Persuasion		×	
Public Speaking		×	
Verbal Clarity		×	
Written Clarity			×
COMPUTER SKILLS:			
Application			×
Expertise			×
SPECIALIZED SKILLS:			
Advanced Degree	×		
Technical School		×	
OJT			×
ATTITUDINAL:			
Positive	×		
Outgoing	×		
Tenacious			×

Career Profile

Career Personality Profile Group: SUPPORTER
Occupation: Counselor

Skill Scoring: (Check)	Non-essential	Useful	Essential
MANAGEMENT:	0, 1, 2	3	4, 5
Administrative		×	
Delegation	×		
Financial	×		
Leadership		×	
Marketing		×	
Motivation		×	
Production	×		
Project Management	×		
Time Management		×	
Training Others	×		
COMMUNICATION:			
Listening			×
Negotiation		×	
Persuasion			×
Public Speaking		×	
Verbal Clarity			×
Written Clarity		×	
COMPUTER SKILLS:			
Application	×		
Expertise	×		
SPECIALIZED SKILLS:			
Advanced Degree		×	
Technical School	×		
OJT		×	
ATTITUDINAL:			
Positive		×	
Outgoing		×	
Tenacious		×	

Career Profile

Career Personality Profile Group: DIRECTOR
Occupation: CPA—Manager/Partner

Skill Scoring: (Check)	Non-essential	Useful	Essential
MANAGEMENT:	0, 1, 2	3	4, 5
Administrative	____	____	✕
Delegation	____	____	✕
Financial	____	____	✕
Leadership	____	✕	____
Marketing	____	✕	____
Motivation	____	✕	____
Production	✕	____	____
Project Management	____	____	✕
Time Management	____	____	✕
Training Others	____	✕	____
COMMUNICATION:			
Listening	____	____	✕
Negotiation	____	____	✕
Persuasion	____	____	✕
Public Speaking	____	✕	____
Verbal Clarity	____	____	✕
Written Clarity	____	____	✕
COMPUTER SKILLS:			
Application	____	____	✕
Expertise	✕	____	____
SPECIALIZED SKILLS:			
Advanced Degree	____	____	✕
Technical School	✕	____	____
OJT	____	✕	____
ATTITUDINAL:			
Positive	____	✕	____
Outgoing	____	✕	____
Tenacious	____	____	✕

Career Profile

Career Personality Profile Group: DIRECTOR
Occupation: <u>Doctor/Dentist</u>

Skill Scoring: (Check)	Non-essential	Useful	Essential
MANAGEMENT:	0, 1, 2	3	4, 5
Administrative		×	
Delegation		×	
Financial			×
Leadership		×	
Marketing			×
Motivation			×
Production	×		
Project Management	×		
Time Management			×
Training Others		×	
COMMUNICATION:			
Listening			×
Negotiation		×	
Persuasion			×
Public Speaking		×	
Verbal Clarity			×
Written Clarity		×	
COMPUTER SKILLS:			
Application		×	
Expertise	×		
SPECIALIZED SKILLS:			
Advanced Degree			×
Technical School	×		
OJT		×	
ATTITUDINAL:			
Positive		×	
Outgoing		×	
Tenacious			×

Career Profile

Career Personality Profile Group: ANALYTICAL
Occupation: Drafter

Skill Scoring: (Check)	Non-essential	Useful	Essential
MANAGEMENT:	0, 1, 2	3	4, 5
Administrative	✕	___	___
Delegation	✕	___	___
Financial	✕	___	___
Leadership	✕	___	___
Marketing	✕	___	___
Motivation	✕	___	___
Production	✕	___	___
Project Management	___	___	✕
Time Management	___	___	✕
Training Others	___	✕	___
COMMUNICATION:			
Listening	___	___	✕
Negotiation	___	✕	___
Persuasion	___	✕	___
Public Speaking	___	✕	___
Verbal Clarity	___	___	✕
Written Clarity	___	✕	___
COMPUTER SKILLS:			
Application	___	___	✕
Expertise	✕	___	___
SPECIALIZED SKILLS:			
Advanced Degree	✕	___	___
Technical School	___	___	✕
OJT	___	✕	___
ATTITUDINAL:			
Positive	___	✕	___
Outgoing	✕	___	___
Tenacious	___	✕	___

Career Profile

Career Personality Profile Group: ANALYTICAL
Occupation: <u>Economist</u>

Skill Scoring: (Check)	Non-essential	Useful	Essential
MANAGEMENT:	0, 1, 2	3	4, 5
Administrative		×	
Delegation	×		
Financial			×
Leadership		×	
Marketing		×	
Motivation		×	
Production	×		
Project Management		×	
Time Management			×
Training Others		×	
COMMUNICATION:			
Listening			×
Negotiation		×	
Persuasion			×
Public Speaking		×	
Verbal Clarity			×
Written Clarity			×
COMPUTER SKILLS:			
Application			×
Expertise	×		
SPECIALIZED SKILLS:			
Advanced Degree			×
Technical School	×		
OJT		×	
ATTITUDINAL:			
Positive	×		
Outgoing		×	
Tenacious			×

Career Profile

Career Personality Profile Group: ANALYTICAL
Occupation: Electronics Engineer

Skill Scoring: (Check)	Non-essential	Useful	Essential
MANAGEMENT:	0, 1, 2	3	4, 5
Administrative	___	×	___
Delegation	___	×	___
Financial	×	___	___
Leadership	___	×	___
Marketing	×	___	___
Motivation	×	___	___
Production	×	___	___
Project Management	___	___	×
Time Management	___	___	×
Training Others	×	___	___
COMMUNICATION:			
Listening	___	___	×
Negotiation	___	×	___
Persuasion	___	×	___
Public Speaking	___	×	___
Verbal Clarity	___	×	___
Written Clarity	___	×	___
COMPUTER SKILLS:			
Application	___	___	×
Expertise	___	×	___
SPECIALIZED SKILLS:			
Advanced Degree	___	×	___
Technical School	___	×	___
OJT	___	×	___
ATTITUDINAL:			
Positive	___	×	___
Outgoing	×	___	___
Tenacious	___	___	×

Career Profile

Career Personality Profile Group: DIRECTOR
Occupation: Entreprenuer

Skill Scoring: (Check)	Non-essential	Useful	Essential
MANAGEMENT:	0, 1, 2	3	4, 5
Administrative		×	
Delegation		×	
Financial			×
Leadership			×
Marketing			×
Motivation			×
Production		×	
Project Management		×	
Time Management			×
Training Others		×	
COMMUNICATION:			
Listening			×
Negotiation			×
Persuasion			×
Public Speaking		×	
Verbal Clarity			×
Written Clarity		×	
COMPUTER SKILLS:			
Application			×
Expertise	×		
SPECIALIZED SKILLS:			
Advanced Degree	×		
Technical School	×		
OJT		×	
ATTITUDINAL:			
Positive			×
Outgoing			×
Tenacious			×

Career Profile

Career Personality Profile Group: ANALYTICAL
Occupation: Forester/Conservationist

Skill Scoring: (Check)	Non-essential	Useful	Essential
MANAGEMENT:	0, 1, 2	3	4, 5
Administrative		✕	
Delegation	✕		
Financial	✕		
Leadership		✕	
Marketing	✕		
Motivation		✕	
Production	✕		
Project Management		✕	
Time Management			✕
Training Others		✕	
COMMUNICATION:			
Listening			✕
Negotiation		✕	
Persuasion			✕
Public Speaking		✕	
Verbal Clarity			✕
Written Clarity			✕
COMPUTER SKILLS:			
Application		✕	
Expertise	✕		
SPECIALIZED SKILLS:			
Advanced Degree		✕	
Technical School	✕		
OJT		✕	
ATTITUDINAL:			
Positive		✕	
Outgoing		✕	
Tenacious			✕

Career Profile

Career Personality Profile Group: ENTERTAINER
Occupation: Graphic Artist

Skill Scoring: (Check)	Non-essential	Useful	Essential
MANAGEMENT:	0, 1, 2	3	4, 5
Administrative		×	
Delegation	×		
Financial	×		
Leadership		×	
Marketing		×	
Motivation		×	
Production		×	
Project Management		×	
Time Management		×	
Training Others		×	
COMMUNICATION:			
Listening		×	
Negotiation		×	
Persuasion		×	
Public Speaking		×	
Verbal Clarity			×
Written Clarity		×	
COMPUTER SKILLS:			
Application		×	
Expertise	×		
SPECIALIZED SKILLS:			
Advanced Degree	×		
Technical School		×	
OJT		×	
ATTITUDINAL:			
Positive		×	
Outgoing			×
Tenacious			×

Career Profile

Career Personality Profile Group: DIRECTOR
Occupation: Health Services Manager

Skill Scoring: (Check)	Non-essential	Useful	Essential
MANAGEMENT:	0, 1, 2	3	4, 5
Administrative	___	___	×
Delegation	___	___	×
Financial	___	___	×
Leadership	___	___	×
Marketing	___	___	×
Motivation	___	___	×
Production	×	___	___
Project Management	___	×	___
Time Management	___	___	×
Training Others	___	×	___
COMMUNICATION:			
Listening	___	___	×
Negotiation	___	___	×
Persuasion	___	___	×
Public Speaking	___	×	___
Verbal Clarity	___	___	×
Written Clarity	___	×	___
COMPUTER SKILLS:			
Application	___	___	×
Expertise	×	___	___
SPECIALIZED SKILLS:			
Advanced Degree	___	×	___
Technical School	___	×	___
OJT	___	×	___
ATTITUDINAL:			
Positive	___	___	×
Outgoing	___	___	×
Tenacious	___	___	×

Career Profile

Career Personality Profile Group: ENTERTAINER
Occupation: <u>Hotel Manager</u>

Skill Scoring: (Check)	Non-essential	Useful	Essential
MANAGEMENT:	0, 1, 2	3	4, 5
Administrative	——	——	×
Delegation	——	——	×
Financial	——	——	×
Leadership	——	——	×
Marketing	——	——	×
Motivation	——	——	×
Production	×	——	——
Project Management	——	×	——
Time Management	——	——	×
Training Others	——	×	——
COMMUNICATION:			
Listening	——	——	×
Negotiation	——	——	×
Persuasion	——	——	×
Public Speaking	——	×	——
Verbal Clarity	——	——	×
Written Clarity	——	×	——
COMPUTER SKILLS:			
Application	——	×	——
Expertise	×	——	——
SPECIALIZED SKILLS:			
Advanced Degree	——	×	——
Technical School	——	——	×
OJT	——	——	×
ATTITUDINAL:			
Positive	——	×	——
Outgoing	——	——	×
Tenacious	——	——	×

Career Profile

Career Personality Profile Group: ANALYTICAL
Occupation: Industrial Engineer

Skill Scoring: (Check)	Non-essential	Useful	Essential
MANAGEMENT:	0, 1, 2	3	4, 5
Administrative			×
Delegation		×	
Financial	×		
Leadership		×	
Marketing	×		
Motivation		×	
Production			×
Project Management			×
Time Management			×
Training Others		×	
COMMUNICATION:			
Listening			×
Negotiation			×
Persuasion			×
Public Speaking		×	
Verbal Clarity			×
Written Clarity			×
COMPUTER SKILLS:			
Application			×
Expertise	×		
SPECIALIZED SKILLS:			
Advanced Degree	×		
Technical School		×	
OJT		×	
ATTITUDINAL:			
Positive		×	
Outgoing		×	
Tenacious			×

Career Profile

Career Personality Profile Group: DIRECTOR
Occupation: <u>Labor Relations Specialist</u>

Skill Scoring: (Check)	Non-essential	Useful	Essential
MANAGEMENT:	0, 1, 2	3	4, 5
Administrative		×	
Delegation	×		
Financial		×	
Leadership			×
Marketing	×		
Motivation			×
Production	×		
Project Management	×		
Time Management			×
Training Others			×
COMMUNICATION:			
Listening			×
Negotiation			×
Persuasion			×
Public Speaking		×	
Verbal Clarity			×
Written Clarity		×	
COMPUTER SKILLS:			
Application		×	
Expertise	×		
SPECIALIZED SKILLS:			
Advanced Degree	×		
Technical School	×		
OJT		×	
ATTITUDINAL:			
Positive		×	
Outgoing		×	
Tenacious			×

Career Profile

Career Personality Profile Group: DIRECTOR
Occupation: Lawyer

Skill Scoring: (Check)	Non-essential	Useful	Essential
MANAGEMENT:	0, 1, 2	3	4, 5
Administrative			×
Delegation			×
Financial		×	
Leadership		×	
Marketing			×
Motivation			×
Production	×		
Project Management		×	
Time Management			×
Training Others		×	
COMMUNICATION:			
Listening			×
Negotiation			×
Persuasion			×
Public Speaking			×
Verbal Clarity			×
Written Clarity		×	
COMPUTER SKILLS:			
Application		×	
Expertise	×		
SPECIALIZED SKILLS:			
Advanced Degree			×
Technical School		×	
OJT		×	
ATTITUDINAL:			
Positive		×	
Outgoing		×	
Tenacious			×

Career Profile

Career Personality Profile Group: SUPPORTER
Occupation: <u>Librarian</u>

Skill Scoring: (Check)	Non-essential	Useful	Essential
MANAGEMENT:	0, 1, 2	3	4, 5
Administrative			×
Delegation		×	
Financial	×		
Leadership	×		
Marketing	×		
Motivation	×		
Production	×		
Project Management	×		
Time Management		×	
Training Others		×	
COMMUNICATION:			
Listening		×	
Negotiation	×		
Persuasion	×		
Public Speaking		×	
Verbal Clarity		×	
Written Clarity		×	
COMPUTER SKILLS:			
Application			×
Expertise	×		
SPECIALIZED SKILLS:			
Advanced Degree		×	
Technical School		×	
OJT		×	
ATTITUDINAL:			
Positive		×	
Outgoing		×	
Tenacious	×		

Career Profile

Career Personality Profile Group: DIRECTOR
Occupation: Long-haul Truck Driver/Owner

Skill Scoring: (Check)	Non-essential	Useful	Essential
MANAGEMENT:	0, 1, 2	3	4, 5
Administrative	____	✕	____
Delegation	____	✕	____
Financial	____	____	✕
Leadership	____	✕	____
Marketing	____	✕	____
Motivation	____	✕	____
Production	____	✕	____
Project Management	✕	____	____
Time Management	____	✕	____
Training Others	✕	____	____
COMMUNICATION:			
Listening	____	✕	____
Negotiation	____	____	✕
Persuasion	____	✕	____
Public Speaking	✕	____	____
Verbal Clarity	____	✕	____
Written Clarity	✕	____	____
COMPUTER SKILLS:			
Application	____	✕	____
Expertise	✕	____	____
SPECIALIZED SKILLS:			
Advanced Degree	✕	____	____
Technical School	____	____	✕
OJT	____	____	✕
ATTITUDINAL:			
Positive	____	✕	____
Outgoing	____	✕	____
Tenacious	____	____	✕

Career Profile

Career Personality Profile Group: ANALYTICAL
Occupation: <u>Market Researcher</u>

Skill Scoring: (Check)	Non-essential	Useful	Essential
MANAGEMENT:	0, 1, 2	3	4, 5
Administrative			×
Delegation		×	
Financial		×	
Leadership	×		
Marketing			×
Motivation			×
Production	×		
Project Management		×	
Time Management			×
Training Others		×	
COMMUNICATION:			
Listening			×
Negotiation		×	
Persuasion			×
Public Speaking		×	
Verbal Clarity			×
Written Clarity			×
COMPUTER SKILLS:			
Application			×
Expertise	×		
SPECIALIZED SKILLS:			
Advanced Degree		×	
Technical School	×		
OJT		×	
ATTITUDINAL:			
Positive		×	
Outgoing		×	
Tenacious			×

Career Profile

Career Personality Profile Group: SUPPORTER
Occupation: Nurse

Skill Scoring: (Check)	Non-essential	Useful	Essential
MANAGEMENT:	0, 1, 2	3	4, 5
Administrative			✕
Delegation		✕	
Financial	✕		
Leadership		✕	
Marketing	✕		
Motivation		✕	
Production	✕		
Project Management	✕		
Time Management			✕
Training Others		✕	
COMMUNICATION:			
Listening			✕
Negotiation		✕	
Persuasion			✕
Public Speaking		✕	
Verbal Clarity			✕
Written Clarity			✕
COMPUTER SKILLS:			
Application			✕
Expertise	✕		
SPECIALIZED SKILLS:			
Advanced Degree		✕	
Technical School			✕
OJT		✕	
ATTITUDINAL:			
Positive			✕
Outgoing		✕	
Tenacious			✕

Career Profile

Career Personality Profile Group: SUPPORTER
Occupation: Occupational Therapist

Skill Scoring: (Check)	Non-essential	Useful	Essential
MANAGEMENT:	0, 1, 2	3	4, 5
Administrative		×	
Delegation	×		
Financial	×		
Leadership		×	
Marketing	×		
Motivation		×	
Production	×		
Project Management	×		
Time Management		×	
Training Others		×	
COMMUNICATION:			
Listening			×
Negotiation		×	
Persuasion			×
Public Speaking		×	
Verbal Clarity			×
Written Clarity		×	
COMPUTER SKILLS:			
Application		×	
Expertise	×		
SPECIALIZED SKILLS:			
Advanced Degree		×	
Technical School	×		
OJT		×	
ATTITUDINAL:			
Positive			×
Outgoing		×	
Tenacious			×

Career Profile

Career Personality Profile Group: SUPPORTER
Occupation: Personnel Specialist

Skill Scoring: (Check)	Non-essential	Useful	Essential
MANAGEMENT:	0, 1, 2	3	4, 5
Administrative			×
Delegation		×	
Financial		×	
Leadership		×	
Marketing		×	
Motivation			×
Production	×		
Project Management		×	
Time Management			×
Training Others		×	
COMMUNICATION:			
Listening			×
Negotiation			×
Persuasion			×
Public Speaking		×	
Verbal Clarity			×
Written Clarity			×
COMPUTER SKILLS:			
Application		×	
Expertise	×		
SPECIALIZED SKILLS:			
Advanced Degree		×	
Technical School	×		
OJT		×	
ATTITUDINAL:			
Positive		×	
Outgoing		×	
Tenacious			×

Career Profile

Career Personality Profile Group: DIRECTOR
Occupation: <u>Police Officer</u>

Skill Scoring: (Check)	Non-essential	Useful	Essential
MANAGEMENT:	0, 1, 2	3	4, 5
Administrative		×	
Delegation	×		
Financial	×		
Leadership		×	
Marketing		×	
Motivation		×	
Production	×		
Project Management	×		
Time Management			×
Training Others		×	
COMMUNICATION:			
Listening			×
Negotiation			×
Persuasion			×
Public Speaking		×	
Verbal Clarity			×
Written Clarity		×	
COMPUTER SKILLS:			
Application		×	
Expertise	×		
SPECIALIZED SKILLS:			
Advanced Degree	×		
Technical School			×
OJT		×	
ATTITUDINAL:			
Positive		×	
Outgoing		×	
Tenacious			×

Career Profile

Career Personality Profile Group: SUPPORTER
Occupation: Psychologist

Skill Scoring: (Check)	Non-essential	Useful	Essential
MANAGEMENT:	0, 1, 2	3	4, 5
Administrative		×	
Delegation		×	
Financial	×		
Leadership		×	
Marketing	×		
Motivation			×
Production	×		
Project Management	×		
Time Management			×
Training Others		×	
COMMUNICATION:			
Listening			×
Negotiation		×	
Persuasion			×
Public Speaking		×	
Verbal Clarity			×
Written Clarity			×
COMPUTER SKILLS:			
Application		×	
Expertise	×		
SPECIALIZED SKILLS:			
Advanced Degree		×	
Technical School	×		
OJT		×	
ATTITUDINAL:			
Positive		×	
Outgoing		×	
Tenacious			×

Career Profile

Career Personality Profile Group: ENTERTAINER
Occupation: Public Relations Specialist

Skill Scoring: (Check)	Non-essential	Useful	Essential
MANAGEMENT:	0, 1, 2	3	4, 5
Administrative	___	×	___
Delegation	___	×	___
Financial	___	×	___
Leadership	___	×	___
Marketing	___	___	×
Motivation	___	___	×
Production	×	___	___
Project Management	___	×	___
Time Management	___	___	×
Training Others	___	×	___
COMMUNICATION:			
Listening	___	___	×
Negotiation	___	×	___
Persuasion	___	___	×
Public Speaking	___	___	×
Verbal Clarity	___	___	×
Written Clarity	___	___	×
COMPUTER SKILLS:			
Application	___	×	___
Expertise	×	___	___
SPECIALIZED SKILLS:			
Advanced Degree	___	×	___
Technical School	×	___	___
OJT	___	×	___
ATTITUDINAL:			
Positive	___	___	×
Outgoing	___	___	×
Tenacious	___	___	×

Career Profile

Career Personality Profile Group: SUPPORTER
Occupation: Radiology Technologist

Skill Scoring: (Check)	Non-essential	Useful	Essential
MANAGEMENT:	0, 1, 2	3	4, 5
Administrative		×	
Delegation	×		
Financial	×		
Leadership	×		
Marketing	×		
Motivation		×	
Production	×		
Project Management	×		
Time Management		×	
Training Others	×		
COMMUNICATION:			
Listening			×
Negotiation	×		
Persuasion		×	
Public Speaking		×	
Verbal Clarity		×	
Written Clarity		×	
COMPUTER SKILLS:			
Application			×
Expertise	×		
SPECIALIZED SKILLS:			
Advanced Degree	×		
Technical School		×	
OJT		×	
ATTITUDINAL:			
Positive		×	
Outgoing	×		
Tenacious		×	

Career Profile

Career Personality Profile Group: DIRECTOR
Occupation: Reporter/Journalist

Skill Scoring: (Check)	Non-essential	Useful	Essential
MANAGEMENT:	0, 1, 2	3	4, 5
Administrative		×	
Delegation	×		
Financial	×		
Leadership		×	
Marketing		×	
Motivation			×
Production	×		
Project Management		×	
Time Management			×
Training Others		×	
COMMUNICATION:			
Listening			×
Negotiation		×	
Persuasion			×
Public Speaking			×
Verbal Clarity			×
Written Clarity			×
COMPUTER SKILLS:			
Application			×
Expertise	×		
SPECIALIZED SKILLS:			
Advanced Degree	×		
Technical School	×		
OJT			×
ATTITUDINAL:			
Positive		×	
Outgoing			×
Tenacious			×

Career Profile

Career Personality Profile Group: DIRECTOR
Occupation: Retail Owner/Manager

Skill Scoring: (Check)	Non-essential	Useful	Essential
MANAGEMENT:	0, 1, 2	3	4, 5
Administrative		×	
Delegation			×
Financial			×
Leadership			×
Marketing			×
Motivation			×
Production	×		
Project Management	×		
Time Management			×
Training Others			×
COMMUNICATION:			
Listening			×
Negotiation		×	
Persuasion			×
Public Speaking		×	
Verbal Clarity			×
Written Clarity		×	
COMPUTER SKILLS:			
Application		×	
Expertise	×		
SPECIALIZED SKILLS:			
Advanced Degree	×		
Technical School	×		
OJT		×	
ATTITUDINAL:			
Positive		×	
Outgoing			×
Tenacious			×

Career Profile

Career Personality Profile Group: ENTERTAINER
Occupation: <u>Salesperson</u>

Skill Scoring: (Check)	Non-essential	Useful	Essential
MANAGEMENT:	0, 1, 2	3	4, 5
Administrative	—		×
Delegation	—	×	
Financial	—	×	
Leadership	—	×	
Marketing	—		×
Motivation	—		×
Production	×		
Project Management	—	×	
Time Management	—		×
Training Others	—	×	
COMMUNICATION:			
Listening	—		×
Negotiation	—		×
Persuasion	—		×
Public Speaking	—		×
Verbal Clarity	—		×
Written Clarity	—		×
COMPUTER SKILLS:			
Application		×	
Expertise	×		
SPECIALIZED SKILLS:			
Advanced Degree	×		
Technical School	×		
OJT	—	×	
ATTITUDINAL:			
Positive	—		×
Outgoing	—		×
Tenacious	—		×

Career Profile

Career Personality Profile Group: SUPPORTER
Occupation: Social Worker

Skill Scoring: (Check)	Non-essential	Useful	Essential
MANAGEMENT:	0, 1, 2	3	4, 5
Administrative			×
Delegation		×	
Financial	×		
Leadership		×	
Marketing	×		
Motivation			×
Production	×		
Project Management		×	
Time Management			×
Training Others		×	
COMMUNICATION:			
Listening			×
Negotiation		×	
Persuasion			×
Public Speaking		×	
Verbal Clarity			×
Written Clarity		×	
COMPUTER SKILLS:			
Application		×	
Expertise	×		
SPECIALIZED SKILLS:			
Advanced Degree		×	
Technical School	×		
OJT		×	
ATTITUDINAL:			
Positive		×	
Outgoing	×		
Tenacious			×

Career Profile

Career Personality Profile Group: ENTERTAINER
Occupation: <u>Stockbroker</u>

Skill Scoring: (Check)	Non-essential	Useful	Essential
MANAGEMENT:	0, 1, 2	3	4, 5
Administrative			×
Delegation	×		
Financial			×
Leadership		×	
Marketing			×
Motivation			×
Production	×		
Project Management	×		
Time Management			×
Training Others	×		
COMMUNICATION:			
Listening			×
Negotiation			×
Persuasion			×
Public Speaking		×	
Verbal Clarity			×
Written Clarity		×	
COMPUTER SKILLS:			
Application			×
Expertise	×		
SPECIALIZED SKILLS:			
Advanced Degree	×		
Technical School			×
OJT			×
ATTITUDINAL:			
Positive		×	
Outgoing			×
Tenacious			×

Career Profile

Career Personality Profile Group: SUPPORTER
Occupation: Teacher/Professor

Skill Scoring: (Check)	Non-essential	Useful	Essential
MANAGEMENT:	0, 1, 2	3	4, 5
Administrative			×
Delegation		×	
Financial	×		
Leadership		×	
Marketing	×		
Motivation		×	
Production	×		
Project Management	×		
Time Management			×
Training Others			×
COMMUNICATION:			
Listening			×
Negotiation		×	
Persuasion			×
Public Speaking			×
Verbal Clarity			×
Written Clarity			×
COMPUTER SKILLS:			
Application		×	
Expertise	×		
SPECIALIZED SKILLS:			
Advanced Degree			×
Technical School	×		
OJT		×	
ATTITUDINAL:			
Positive		×	
Outgoing			×
Tenacious			×

Career Profile

Career Personality Profile Group: ENTERTAINER
Occupation: Travel Agent

Skill Scoring: (Check)	Non-essential	Useful	Essential
MANAGEMENT:	0, 1, 2	3	4, 5
Administrative		×	
Delegation	×		
Financial		×	
Leadership		×	
Marketing			×
Motivation			×
Production	×		
Project Management	×		
Time Management			×
Training Others	×		
COMMUNICATION:			
Listening			×
Negotiation		×	
Persuasion			×
Public Speaking		×	
Verbal Clarity			×
Written Clarity		×	
COMPUTER SKILLS:			
Application			×
Expertise	×		
SPECIALIZED SKILLS:			
Advanced Degree	×		
Technical School		×	
OJT			×
ATTITUDINAL:			
Positive		×	
Outgoing			×
Tenacious			×

Career Profile

Career Personality Profile Group: ANALYTICAL
Occupation: Underwriter

Skill Scoring: (Check)	Non-essential	Useful	Essential
MANAGEMENT:	0, 1, 2	3	4, 5
Administrative	___	___	×
Delegation	___	×	___
Financial	___	___	×
Leadership	___	×	___
Marketing	___	×	___
Motivation	___	×	___
Production	×	___	___
Project Management	×	___	___
Time Management	___	___	×
Training Others	___	×	___
COMMUNICATION:			
Listening	___	×	___
Negotiation	___	×	___
Persuasion	___	×	___
Public Speaking	×	___	___
Verbal Clarity	___	×	___
Written Clarity	___	×	___
COMPUTER SKILLS:			
Application	___	___	×
Expertise	×	___	___
SPECIALIZED SKILLS:			
Advanced Degree	×	___	___
Technical School	×	___	___
OJT	___	×	___
ATTITUDINAL:			
Positive	×	___	___
Outgoing	×	___	___
Tenacious	___	×	___

Chapter 5

How to Change Jobs, Industries, or Career Fields

CHOICES, CHOICES, CHOICES. It's almost like being a kid again. Here you are, an adult, having worked for a number of years, now facing many of the same choices you had when you first graduated. The difference is that now you have a lot more experience and obligations. You also may feel your choice is more important now; you have less time to recover from a mistake. Now you must put forth the effort to make a good decision and achieve success.

All Mid-Career Changes Are Not Alike

Up to this point, you have had the opportunity to assess the security of your job and to recognize the effect that values have on job satisfaction. You have been able to appraise your knowledge and skills and see how they can be transferred to other career fields while retaining your career equity. This chapter's objective is to help you understand the effort, time, and dollars required to make any one of the four different changes available to mid-career people. These changes are:

1. Change job and stay with the same company.
2. Change job and company, but stay in the same industry.
3. Change job, staying in the same profession, but change industry.
4. Change profession and industry.

Each of these four changes requires a different level of time, money, and effort. Your time investment can be as little as a few months or more than a year. Your dollar investment can range from nothing to more than $25,000, depending upon what you choose to do. By recognizing the differences, you can weigh your emotional needs against your time and financial needs to determine which change is best for you.

The Job, Industry, & Career Change Guide on page 108 gives you a quick way to comprehend the differences between each change. The remainder of this chapter describes the issues unique to each of the four changes.

Job Change: Same Company, Same Career

After studying the guide, you can see that the easiest change to make is that of transferring within your present company. Moving from one department or division to another requires that you take the time to assess your skills. Then make it known within the company that you are looking for a change. To enhance your effort, attend in-house training programs or outside seminars where you will meet new people who can assist you in your networking.

As you can see on the chart, the cost and time required for such a change is minimal; rarely should such a change exceed $500.

Yet the reward can be great. You may get the chance to

broaden your skills, gain new responsibility, or increase your overall knowledge of the company. You may be happy with your present company but have stress due to a values conflict with your boss. This type of change eliminates that problem and allows you to stay with the company.

Job Change: Same Industry, Same Career

This second change requires more effort, time, and money than the first one. Changing jobs within the same industry enables you to keep your career equity. Your senior knowledge will be easily recognized by a prospective employer.

As you can see from the chart, you need to develop a marketing plan (see Chapter 10) and to network with others in the industry. We also recommend working with a professional recruiter who specializes in your industry. Remember, a recruiter costs you nothing; their fee is paid by the hiring employer. The cost of this type of change should not exceed $1,000 unless you decide to go to an industry conference that is located at an expensive resort.

This type of change will offer you the opportunity to find a company that more closely meets your values standard. Also, very often a mid-career change of this kind results in a promotion and pay increase.

Industry Change: Same Career

Now the real work begins. Your challenge in an industry career change, as we discussed in Chapter 4, is keeping your career equity. It will be very important that you follow the directions on the chart. Make sure you understand how to convey the value of your transferable skills to a prospective employer; if it is not clear to you, reread Chapter 4.

You can see from the chart that this change requires considerable money and effort, but the rewards are equal to the investment. One of your first steps is to join the trade association for your target industry. We strongly recommend that you attend the industry's national conference. This will

Job, Industry, & Career Change Guide

	Job Change: Same Company Same Career	Job Change: Same Industry Same Career	Industry Change: Same Career	Career Field Change
REQUIRED EFFORT	• Assess skills • Network in company • Apply for posted job openings	• Assess skills • Update resume • Develop marketing plan • Network in industry • Work with a recruiter • Apply for advertised positions	• Assess skills • Update resume • Develop marketing plan • Network in target industry • Work with a recruiter • Join target industry/trade associations • Apply for advertised positions • Complete training/education unique to target industry	• Assess skills • Assess risk/tolerance • Select target career • Develop marketing plan • Evaluate competition • Meet training/education requirements • Join target industry/trade associations • Apply for advertised positions • Attend industry conference
OPTIONAL EFFORT	• Complete education • Attend in-house training • Attend skill enhancement seminars • Update and distribute resume	• Look outside local area • Complete education • Attend skill enhancement seminars • Attend industry conference	• Look outside local area • Attend industry conference	• Look outside local area • Work with a recruiter • Buy a business

REQUIRED INVESTMENT			
• 0–$100 resume • $100+ networking • $100–$500 seminars	• 0–$100 resume • $100–$200 assoc. dues • $100+ networking	• 0–$100 resume • $100–$200 assoc. dues • $100+ networking • $500+ training/education	• 0–$100 resume • $100–$200 assoc. dues • $100+ networking • $500+ industry conference • $500+ training/education
OPTIONAL INVESTMENT			
	• $100–$500 seminars • $500+ industry conference • $500+ training/education	• $500+ industry conference	• $25,000+ buy/start business
REQUIRED TIME TO COMPLETE			
• 1 to 6 months	• 1 month for each $10,000 of income	• 1 month for each $10,000 of income • Plus 1 to 6 months industry familiarization	• Probable minimum of 1 year training or education • 1 month for each $10,000 of income • 1 to 2 years with no income if you start your own business

increase your costs, but greatly improve your chances of finding a plum job.

As a mid-career changer, you can enter a new industry, quickly establish a credible reputation using your experience, and then move ahead.

Career Field Change

A career field change is the most difficult to make. It often results in starting a business of your own. Mid-career changers are the primary prospects for people who sell business franchises. Today there are about 3,100 different franchises in 60 different industries. The choices are fantastic. The range of investment can be as low as $25,000 and as high as $250,000. Experts say that most good franchise opportunities are available between $25,000 and $50,000.

Before you go very far with a change in career fields, be sure to assess your willingness to take both financial and emotional risks. As you can see, there's a high cost in time and money when changing career fields, and there's a good chance your change won't work out as planned. The grass-is-greener delusion is the primary cause of such failure. Too often people have a romantic ideal of a different career field. Once they enter that field, they find that many of the problems they wanted to leave behind still exist, plus additional ones.

To assess your risk tolerance, make a list of all the things that could go wrong with a career change and the possible solutions to those consequences. Then list the benefits you realize if you do take the risks and do succeed. Do the benefits outweigh the consequences? Are the benefits great enough that you can tolerate taking the risks?

To validate your list, talk with someone who made a similar change or who works in your target career field. Ask them if your assessment is realistic and if you have accurately weighed the consequences and benefits.

Then determine what your next step should be. Do you go on with this career change or do you step back and select an alternative?

* * *

This chapter gave you some points to consider in charting a direction for your career change. The greater the change you make in your career, the more effort required for its success and the bigger the risks. The next chapter will help you answer an important question. What is your earning potential? That's always a fun thing to learn about and will greatly influence the final choice you make.

Chapter 6

There's Gold in Those Skills

EVERY PERSON we have met going through a mid-career crisis has one burning question on their mind: "How much am I worth if I change jobs or careers?" This chapter gives you the best answer you can get, short of receiving an actual job offer.

Kent is a typical mid-career changer. As director of labor relations (executive management), he received eight promotions during his sixteen years with a Fortune 500 company. His skill as a labor relations negotiator was so effective that he saved his company $100 million per year on just one labor contract.

A corporate takeover changed the company culture and Kent became uncomfortable. He wanted to leave. But his salary was just under $90,000 per year, and he was afraid he could not find another job at the same income level. By taking into account his skills, his company's size, and the metropolitan area in which he worked, he learned from the charts at the end of this chapter that he had the potential to earn a higher salary. (See Kent's example on page 119.)

Kent's fast-track career was within one company. Because of this, his merit and promotional raises were *less* than what he would have received on the open market. When Kent came to us, he thought it would be difficult to replace his job due to his high pay level. To his surprise and delight, he learned otherwise. In a large city, within a large company, his annual earning potential was between $124,000 and $153,000.

This new knowledge allowed Kent to examine a career change with greater confidence. It also helped him look at options he had not considered before.

Translating What You Know into Future Value

Discovering your skills is very important; putting a dollar value on them is equally important. Knowing both can help you capitalize on your real potential and realistically evaluate your earnings potential.

Most people equate their worth with how much they are paid. That assessment can be wrong for two primary reasons. You can be **overpaid** because you have been with one company and in one position too long. Or you can be **underpaid** because you have had too many promotions too rapidly within the same company.

How You Get Overpaid

Alice became production manager in 1973. She learned every nuance of the production process under her supervision. She knew the job so well that she didn't "take problems home." She came to work at 7:30 A.M. and clocked out at 4:30 P.M. five days a week. She built a close-knit team that worked like a well-oiled machine. Her company was a union shop, so she consistently received cost-of-living and merit increases to keep pace with the union contracts. She was earning $56,000 per year as a frontline manager.

Actually, her marketable skills were limited. She knew only one business. She had limited knowledge of management skills such as administration, delegation, and financial planning. She worked with a small company in a small metropolitan area.

She decided to make a change because she wanted more of a challenge. Her problem was classic: she had built a life-style around her comfortable income.

Knowing *how much* she was overpaid allowed her to evaluate options more accurately. In order to keep her pay level, she would have to move to a larger community and a larger company. Her other choice was to expand her skills so she could find a better job in the same community.

She decided to expand her skills. By studying the Skills Market Value worksheets in this chapter, she determined what new skills she needed in order to progress in management. Alice is currently attending a junior college studying sales, marketing, and management. She intends to get an associate of arts degree and possibly go on for a bachelor's.

Recognizing how much she was overpaid helped her appreciate her job. Going back to school to broaden her skills added zest to her life.

How You Get Underpaid

Kent is another classic case study. Companies from large to small are filled with successful employees who are underpaid. Employers would have to offer a great deal more money if they recruited outside the company to fill these same positions. At Xerox, for example, some people would leave the company for a few years and later return, receiving a higher salary than their peers who stayed. Xerox employees called this "the compression factor": a company promotes and gives salary increases that become a smaller percentage with each step, until a ceiling is reached. This is done for several reasons. Management wants to have a discernible salary gap between upper and lower management, and they want to keep costs under control wherever possible. Companies get away with it because many people feel comfortable with the company they have "grown up" with.

If you decide to change careers, the compression factor can be an advantage. You'll have no problem with a competitive offer. However, it also means that you must be effective in salary negotiations. Do not fall into the trap of divulging your salary to a potential employer, because if your salary is substantially lower than average, they may reduce the offer.

When you are asked the question "What do you expect to earn on this job?" be sure to answer: "I expect to be paid a competitive rate commensurate with the duties of the job. What is your offer?"

How to Calculate What You Are Worth

According to the *Statistical Abstract of the United States 1990*, the median earnings for executives, administrators, and managerial staff were:

Men = $26,656
Women = $17,606

Those numbers could make you feel overpaid. Remember, a median number means that half the population being tabulated falls below the median number and half the population is above it. Median is not an average.

By contrast, the average senior executive salary according to Korn/Ferry's 1989 *Executive Profile* was $289,000. "Of this amount, $190,000 is base salary and $99,000, bonus." This is more than double the $116,000 reported in 1979. Now you may feel underpaid.

Understanding Pay Variables

Some industries, such as the computer industry, are known for high pay. Others, such as the service industry, are known for low pay. Between 1981 and 1986 there were 12 million new service jobs. Fast-food restaurants and retail stores pay frontline managers as little as $7.00 per hour. If you figure that one frontline manager is needed for every seven service employees, that increase created a lot of low-paying management jobs. By contrast, the pay given to savings and loan executives has been very high in some cases. Somewhere in the middle is the average company.

The worksheets at the end of this chapter are designed to represent the **average** company and its monetary reward for management skills. Your industry could be an exception. For example, if you are in frontline management with a retail company, you may find you are underpaid according to the charts in this chapter. But if you are in executive management with a retail company, you could be overpaid, surprisingly, according to these charts. If you know your industry's pay is exceptional in either direction, take that into consideration once you have computed your earning potential.

In other words, these charts are guides. Don't take them to your boss and demand a pay raise! They can't guarantee the salary offers you will receive from prospective employers, either.

The charts are valuable because they give you *an indication of your potential earning power* and they show you what skills can enhance or detract from your earning potential.

How to Calculate Your Earning Potential

If you have not already filled out the Career Skills Evaluation chart, return to Chapter 4 and do so.

Now take those scores and transfer the information to a Skills Market Value Chart & Worksheet. Turn to the chart that represents the job level, target company size, and the size of the metropolitan area in which you are doing your job search. Transfer your average score for each skill to this chart, checking the appropriate boxes. Remember, you may not have a skill rating for every skill box if you and your friends did an honest evaluation. Even Lee Iacocca would not be skilled in every category.

Next, count from left to right on the graph the same number of shaded boxes as your skill score; put an X in the appropriate box. Determine the low and high dollar value of that skill, and write each dollar value in the columns to the right of the graph. Do this for every applicable skill.

Total the "Low" and "High" value columns. If appropriate, calculate the increased "Attitudinal" factor: multiply each "Market Value Subtotal" figure by .5% for every rating of 4 or

5 you received on "Positive," "Outgoing," or "Tenacious." Add the resulting numbers to the subtotal for your "Total Market Value Range." You now have a picture of your potential **average** earnings based upon your identified skill levels.

For the fun of it, look at the differences in your earning power if you were to increase your level of management, move to a bigger city, or work for a larger company.

Perhaps you are tired of the hassles of a large city, like Los Angeles, and want to move to a smaller one, such as Salem, Oregon. The charts can give you an idea of the difference this would make in your earning potential. This knowledge can greatly improve your planning process.

The examples of Alice's and Kent's charts, on the following pages, can help you understand how to fill out your own charts.

Have fun.

Alice's Example

Skills Market Value Chart & Worksheet

FRONT LINE MANAGEMENT
Small Company (Less than $50 Million)
Small Metro Area (Less than 250,000 Population)

Skills/Score

Management:	(Poor) (Best) 1 2 3 4 5	Low	High
Administrative	☐ ☒ ☐ ☐ ☐	$150	$200
Delegation	☐ ☐ ☒ ☐ ☐	$200	$250
Financial N/A	☐ ☐ ☐ ☐ ☐	$ —	$ —
Leadership	☐ ☐ ☐ ☒ ☐	$425	$525
Marketing N/A	☐ ☐ ☐ ☐ ☐	$ —	$ —
Motivation	☐ ☐ ☒ ☐ ☐	$350	$400
Production	☐ ☐ ☐ ☒ ☐	$400	$450
Project Mgmt. N/A	☐ ☐ ☐ ☐ ☐	$ —	$ —
Time Mgmt.	☐ ☐ ☒ ☐ ☐	$200	$250
Training Others	☐ ☐ ☒ ☐ ☐	$200	$250
Communication:			
Listening	☐ ☐ ☒ ☐ ☐	$350	$400
Negotiation N/A	☐ ☐ ☐ ☐ ☐	$ —	$ —
Persuasion	☐ ☐ ☐ ☒ ☐	$400	$500
Public Speaking N/A	☐ ☐ ☐ ☐ ☐	$ —	$ —
Verbal Clarity	☐ ☐ ☒ ☐ ☐	$200	$250
Written Clarity	☐ ☐ ☒ ☐ ☐	$150	$200
Computer Skills:			
Application Use N/A	☐ ☐ ☐ ☐ ☐	$ —	$ —
Computer Expert N/A	☐ ☐ ☐ ☐ ☐	$ —	$ —
Specialized Skills:			
Advanced Degree N/A	☐ ☐ ☐ ☐ ☐	$ —	$ —
Technical Sch. N/A	☐ ☐ ☐ ☐ ☐	$ —	$ —
O-J-T Training	☐ ☒ ☐ ☐ ☐	$150	$250

Market Value Sub-Total $3175 $3925

Attitudinal:		
Positive	☐ ☐ ☐ ☐ ☐	$ — $ —
Outgoing	☐ ☐ ☐ ☐ ☐	$ — $ —
Tenacious	☐ ☐ ☐ ☐ ☐	$ — $ —

Multiply your total earnings by .5% for each category with a 4 or 5 rating in this section.

Total Market Value Range $3175 $3925
(Monthly Income X 12 for Annual Value)

$38,100 $47,100

Kent's Example

Skills Market Value Chart & Worksheet
EXECUTIVE MANAGEMENT
Large Company ($500 Million+)
Large Metro Area (2 Million+ Population)

Skills/Score

Management:	(Poor) 1 2 3 4 5 (Best)	Low	High
Administrative	☐☐☐☒☐	$450	$575
Delegation	☐☐☐☒☐	$650	$800
Financial	☐☐☒☐☐	$800	$1000
Leadership	☐☐☐☐☒	$1500	$1700
Marketing	☒☐☐☐☐	$700	$850
Motivation	☐☐☐☒☐	$800	$975
Production N/A	☐☐☐☐☐	$—	$—
Project Mgmt.	☐☒☐☐☐	$550	$725
Time Mgmt.	☐☐☒☐☐	$400	$500
Training Others	☐☒☐☐☐	$100	$150

Communication:		Low	High
Listening	☐☐☐☒☐	$500	$700
Negotiation	☐☐☐☐☒	$700	$800
Persuasion	☐☐☒☐☐	$600	$700
Public Speaking	☐☒☐☐☐	$600	$750
Verbal Clarity	☐☐☒☐☐	$750	$825
Written Clarity	☐☐☒☐☐	$300	$400

Computer Skills:		Low	High
Application Use	☐☐☒☐☐	$350	$500
Computer Expert N/A	☐☐☐☐☐	$—	$—

Specialized Skills:		Low	High
Advanced Degree N/A	☐☐☐☐☐	$—	$—
Technical Sch. N/A	☐☐☐☐☐	$—	$—
O-J-T Training	☐☐☐☒☐	$450	$600

Market Value Sub-Total $10,200 $12,550

Attitudinal:			
Positive	☐☐☐☒☐	$51	$63
Outgoing	☐☐☐☒☐	$51	$63
Tenacious	☐☐☐☐☒	$51	$63

Multiply your total earnings by .5% for each category with a 4 or 5 rating in this section.

Total Market Value Range $10,353 $12,739
(Monthly Income X 12 for Annual Value)

$124,236 $152,868

Skills Market Value Chart & Worksheet
EXECUTIVE MANAGEMENT
Large Company ($500 Million+)
Large Metro Area (2 Million+ Population)

Skills/Score

	(Poor) (Best) 1 2 3 4 5	Chart (100–1600)	Low	High
Management:				
Administrative	☐☐☐☐☐		$____	$____
Delegation	☐☐☐☐☐		$____	$____
Financial	☐☐☐☐☐		$____	$____
Leadership	☐☐☐☐☐		$____	$____
Marketing	☐☐☐☐☐		$____	$____
Motivation	☐☐☐☐☐		$____	$____
Production	☐☐☐☐☐		$____	$____
Project Mgmt.	☐☐☐☐☐		$____	$____
Time Mgmt.	☐☐☐☐☐		$____	$____
Training Others	☐☐☐☐☐		$____	$____
Communication:				
Listening	☐☐☐☐☐		$____	$____
Negotiation	☐☐☐☐☐		$____	$____
Persuasion	☐☐☐☐☐		$____	$____
Public Speaking	☐☐☐☐☐		$____	$____
Verbal Clarity	☐☐☐☐☐		$____	$____
Written Clarity	☐☐☐☐☐		$____	$____
Computer Skills:				
Application Use	☐☐☐☐☐		$____	$____
Computer Expert	☐☐☐☐☐		$____	$____
Specialized Skills:				
Advanced Degree	☐☐☐☐☐		$____	$____
Technical Sch.	☐☐☐☐☐		$____	$____
O-J-T Training	☐☐☐☐☐		$____	$____

Market Value Sub-Total $____ $____

Attitudinal:

Positive	☐☐☐☐☐		$____	$____
Outgoing	☐☐☐☐☐	*Multiply your total earnings by .5% for each category with a 4 or 5 rating in this section.*	$____	$____
Tenacious	☐☐☐☐☐		$____	$____

Total Market Value Range $____ $____
(Monthly Income X 12 for Annual Value)

Skills Market Value Chart & Worksheet
EXECUTIVE MANAGEMENT
Large Company ($500 Million +)
Medium Metro Area (250,000 — 2 Million Population)

Skills/Score

	(Poor) (Best) 1 2 3 4 5		Low	High
Management:		100 200 400 600 800 1000 1200 1400 1600		
Administrative	☐☐☐☐☐		$____	$____
Delegation	☐☐☐☐☐		$____	$____
Financial	☐☐☐☐☐		$____	$____
Leadership	☐☐☐☐☐		$____	$____
Marketing	☐☐☐☐☐		$____	$____
Motivation	☐☐☐☐☐		$____	$____
Production	☐☐☐☐☐		$____	$____
Project Mgmt.	☐☐☐☐☐		$____	$____
Time Mgmt.	☐☐☐☐☐		$____	$____
Training Others	☐☐☐☐☐		$____	$____
Communication:				
Listening	☐☐☐☐☐		$____	$____
Negotiation	☐☐☐☐☐		$____	$____
Persuasion	☐☐☐☐☐		$____	$____
Public Speaking	☐☐☐☐☐		$____	$____
Verbal Clarity	☐☐☐☐☐		$____	$____
Written Clarity	☐☐☐☐☐		$____	$____
Computer Skills:				
Application Use	☐☐☐☐☐		$____	$____
Computer Expert	☐☐☐☐☐		$____	$____
Specialized Skills:				
Advanced Degree	☐☐☐☐☐		$____	$____
Technical Sch.	☐☐☐☐☐		$____	$____
O-J-T Training	☐☐☐☐☐		$____	$____

Market Value Sub-Total $____ $____

Attitudinal:

			Low	High
Positive	☐☐☐☐☐		$____	$____
Outgoing	☐☐☐☐☐	*Multiply your total earnings by .5% for each category with a 4 or 5 rating in this section.*	$____	$____
Tenacious	☐☐☐☐☐		$____	$____

Total Market Value Range $____ $____
(Monthly Income X 12 for Annual Value)

Skills Market Value Chart & Worksheet
EXECUTIVE MANAGEMENT
Large Company ($500 Million +)
Small Metro Area (Less than 250,000 Population)

Skills/Score

	(Poor) (Best) 1 2 3 4 5			Low	High
Management:					
Administrative	☐☐☐☐☐			$___	$___
Delegation	☐☐☐☐☐			$___	$___
Financial	☐☐☐☐☐			$___	$___
Leadership	☐☐☐☐☐			$___	$___
Marketing	☐☐☐☐☐			$___	$___
Motivation	☐☐☐☐☐			$___	$___
Production	☐☐☐☐☐			$___	$___
Project Mgmt.	☐☐☐☐☐			$___	$___
Time Mgmt.	☐☐☐☐☐			$___	$___
Training Others	☐☐☐☐☐			$___	$___
Communication:					
Listening	☐☐☐☐☐			$___	$___
Negotiation	☐☐☐☐☐			$___	$___
Persuasion	☐☐☐☐☐			$___	$___
Public Speaking	☐☐☐☐☐			$___	$___
Verbal Clarity	☐☐☐☐☐			$___	$___
Written Clarity	☐☐☐☐☐			$___	$___
Computer Skills:					
Application Use	☐☐☐☐☐			$___	$___
Computer Expert	☐☐☐☐☐			$___	$___
Specialized Skills:					
Advanced Degree	☐☐☐☐☐			$___	$___
Technical Sch.	☐☐☐☐☐			$___	$___
O-J-T Training	☐☐☐☐☐			$___	$___

Chart scale: 100 200 400 600 800 1000 1200 1400 1600

Market Value Sub-Total $___ $___

Attitudinal:

				Low	High
Positive	☐☐☐☐☐			$___	$___
Outgoing	☐☐☐☐☐			$___	$___
Tenacious	☐☐☐☐☐			$___	$___

Multiply your total earnings by .5% for each category with a 4 or 5 rating in this section.

Total Market Value Range $___ $___
(Monthly Income X 12 for Annual Value)

Skills Market Value Chart & Worksheet
EXECUTIVE MANAGEMENT
Medium Company ($50 Million — $500 Million)
Large Metro Area (2 Million+ Population)

Skills/Score

	(Poor) (Best) 1 2 3 4 5		Low	High
Management:	☐☐☐☐☐			
Administrative	☐☐☐☐☐		$____	$____
Delegation	☐☐☐☑☐		$____	$____
Financial	☐☐☐☐☐		$____	$____
Leadership	☐☐☐☐☐		$____	$____
Marketing	☐☐☐☐☐		$____	$____
Motivation	☐☐☐☐☐		$____	$____
Production	☐☐☐☐☐		$____	$____
Project Mgmt.	☐☐☐☐☐		$____	$____
Time Mgmt.	☐☐☐☐☐		$____	$____
Training Others	☐☐☐☐☐		$____	$____
Communication:				
Listening	☐☐☐☐☐			
Negotiation	☐☐☐☐☐		$____	$____
Persuasion	☐☐☐☐☐		$____	$____
Public Speaking	☐☐☐☐☐		$____	$____
Verbal Clarity	☐☐☐☐☐		$____	$____
Written Clarity	☐☐☐☐☐		$____	$____
Computer Skills:				
Application Use	☐☐☐☐☐		$____	$____
Computer Expert	☐☐☐☐☐		$____	$____
Specialized Skills:				
Advanced Degree	☐☐☐☐☐		$____	$____
Technical Sch.	☐☐☐☐☐		$____	$____
O-J-T Training	☐☐☐☐☐		$____	$____

The chart scale reads: 100, 200, 400, 600, 800, 1000, 1200, 1400, 1600

Market Value Sub-Total $____ $____

Attitudinal:

			Low	High
Positive	☐☐☐☐☐		$____	$____
Outgoing	☐☐☐☐☐		$____	$____
Tenacious	☐☐☐☐☐		$____	$____

Multiply your total earnings by .5% for each category with a 4 or 5 rating in this section.

Total Market Value Range $____ $____

(Monthly Income X 12 for Annual Value)

Skills Market Value Chart & Worksheet

EXECUTIVE MANAGEMENT
Medium Company ($50 Million — $500 Million)
Medium Metro Area (250,000 — 2 Million Population)

Skills/Score

	(Poor) (Best) 1 2 3 4 5	Chart	Low	High
Management:		100 200 400 600 800 1000 1200 1400 1600		
Administrative	☐☐☐☐☐		$____	$____
Delegation	☐☐☐☐☐		$____	$____
Financial	☐☐☐☐☐		$____	$____
Leadership	☐☐☐☐☐		$____	$____
Marketing	☐☐☐☐☐		$____	$____
Motivation	☐☐☐☐☐		$____	$____
Production	☐☐☐☐☐		$____	$____
Project Mgmt.	☐☐☐☐☐		$____	$____
Time Mgmt.	☐☐☐☐☐		$____	$____
Training Others	☐☐☐☐☐		$____	$____
Communication:				
Listening	☐☐☐☐☐		$____	$____
Negotiation	☐☐☐☐☐		$____	$____
Persuasion	☐☐☐☐☐		$____	$____
Public Speaking	☐☐☐☐☐		$____	$____
Verbal Clarity	☐☐☐☐☐		$____	$____
Written Clarity	☐☐☐☐☐		$____	$____
Computer Skills:				
Application Use	☐☐☐☐☐		$____	$____
Computer Expert	☐☐☐☐☐		$____	$____
Specialized Skills:				
Advanced Degree	☐☐☐☐☐		$____	$____
Technical Sch.	☐☐☐☐☐		$____	$____
O-J-T Training	☐☐☐☐☐		$____	$____

Market Value Sub-Total $____ $____

Attitudinal:

	1 2 3 4 5		Low	High
Positive	☐☐☐☐☐	*Multiply your total earnings by .5% for each category with a 4 or 5 rating in this section.*	$____	$____
Outgoing	☐☐☐☐☐		$____	$____
Tenacious	☐☐☐☐☐		$____	$____

Total Market Value Range $____ $____
(Monthly Income X 12 for Annual Value)

Skills Market Value Chart & Worksheet
EXECUTIVE MANAGEMENT
Medium Company ($50 Million — $500 Million)
Small Metro Area (Less than 250,000 Population)

Skills/Score

Scale markings: 100 200 400 600 800 1000 1200 1400 1600   Low   High

Management: (Poor) 1 2 3 4 5 (Best)

	Low	High
Administrative	$___	$___
Delegation	$___	$___
Financial	$___	$___
Leadership	$___	$___
Marketing	$___	$___
Motivation	$___	$___
Production	$___	$___
Project Mgmt.	$___	$___
Time Mgmt.	$___	$___
Training Others	$___	$___

Communication:

	Low	High
Listening	$___	$___
Negotiation	$___	$___
Persuasion	$___	$___
Public Speaking	$___	$___
Verbal Clarity	$___	$___
Written Clarity	$___	$___

Computer Skills:

	Low	High
Application Use	$___	$___
Computer Expert	$___	$___

Specialized Skills:

	Low	High
Advanced Degree	$___	$___
Technical Sch.	$___	$___
O-J-T Training	$___	$___

Market Value Sub-Total $_____ $_____

Attitudinal:

Multiply your total earnings by .5% for each category with a 4 or 5 rating in this section.

	Low	High
Positive	$___	$___
Outgoing	$___	$___
Tenacious	$___	$___

Total Market Value Range $_____ $_____
(Monthly Income X 12 for Annual Value)

Skills Market Value Chart & Worksheet
EXECUTIVE MANAGEMENT
Small Company (Less than $50 Million)
Large Metro Area (2 Million + Population)

Skills/Score

	(Poor) (Best) 1 2 3 4 5		Low	High
Management:				
Administrative	☐☐☐☐☐		$____	$____
Delegation	☐☐☐☐☐		$____	$____
Financial	☐☐☐☐☐		$____	$____
Leadership	☐☐☐☐☐		$____	$____
Marketing	☐☐☐☐☐		$____	$____
Motivation	☐☐☐☐☐		$____	$____
Production	☐☐☐☐☐		$____	$____
Project Mgmt.	☐☐☐☐☐		$____	$____
Time Mgmt.	☐☐☐☐☐		$____	$____
Training Others	☐☐☐☐☐		$____	$____
Communication:				
Listening	☐☐☐☐☐		$____	$____
Negotiation	☐☐☐☐☐		$____	$____
Persuasion	☐☐☐☐☐		$____	$____
Public Speaking	☐☐☐☐☐		$____	$____
Verbal Clarity	☐☐☐☐☐		$____	$____
Written Clarity	☐☐☐☐☐		$____	$____
Computer Skills:				
Application Use	☐☐☐☐☐		$____	$____
Computer Expert	☐☐☐☐☐		$____	$____
Specialized Skills:				
Advanced Degree	☐☐☐☐☐		$____	$____
Technical Sch.	☐☐☐☐☐		$____	$____
O-J-T Training	☐☐☐☐☐		$____	$____

Market Value Sub-Total $____ $____

Attitudinal:

			Low	High
Positive	☐☐☐☐☐	*Multiply your total earnings by .5% for*	$____	$____
Outgoing	☐☐☐☐☐	*each category with a 4 or 5 rating in*	$____	$____
Tenacious	☐☐☐☐☐	*this section.*	$____	$____

Total Market Value Range $____ $____
(Monthly Income X 12 for Annual Value)

Skills Market Value Chart & Worksheet
EXECUTIVE MANAGEMENT
Small Company (Less than $50 Million)
Medium Metro Area (250,000 to 2 Million Population)

Skills/Score

Management: (Poor) 1 2 3 4 5 (Best)

Scale: 100 200 400 600 800 1000 1200 1400 1600

Skill	Low	High
Administrative	$____	$____
Delegation	$____	$____
Financial	$____	$____
Leadership	$____	$____
Marketing	$____	$____
Motivation	$____	$____
Production	$____	$____
Project Mgmt.	$____	$____
Time Mgmt.	$____	$____
Training Others	$____	$____

Communication:

Skill	Low	High
Listening	$____	$____
Negotiation	$____	$____
Persuasion	$____	$____
Public Speaking	$____	$____
Verbal Clarity	$____	$____
Written Clarity	$____	$____

Computer Skills:

Skill	Low	High
Application Use	$____	$____
Computer Expert	$____	$____

Specialized Skills:

Skill	Low	High
Advanced Degree	$____	$____
Technical Sch.	$____	$____
O-J-T Training	$____	$____

Market Value Sub-Total $____ $____

Attitudinal:

Skill	Low	High
Positive	$____	$____
Outgoing	$____	$____
Tenacious	$____	$____

Multiply your total earnings by .5% for each category with a 4 or 5 rating in this section.

Total Market Value Range $____ $____

(Monthly Income X 12 for Annual Value)

Skills Market Value Chart & Worksheet

EXECUTIVE MANAGEMENT
Small Company (Less than $50 Million)
Small Metro Area (Less than 250,000 Population)

Skills/Score

	(Poor) (Best) 1 2 3 4 5	100 200 400 600 800 1000 1200 1400 1600	Low	High
Management:				
Administrative	☐☐☐☐☐		$___	$___
Delegation	☐☐☐☐☐		$___	$___
Financial	☐☐☐☐☐		$___	$___
Leadership	☐☐☐☐☐		$___	$___
Marketing	☐☐☐☐☐		$___	$___
Motivation	☐☐☐☐☐		$___	$___
Production	☐☐☐☐☐		$___	$___
Project Mgmt.	☐☐☐☐☐		$___	$___
Time Mgmt.	☐☐☐☐☐		$___	$___
Training Others	☐☐☐☐☐		$___	$___
Communication:				
Listening	☐☐☐☐☐		$___	$___
Negotiation	☐☐☐☐☐		$___	$___
Persuasion	☐☐☐☐☐		$___	$___
Public Speaking	☐☐☐☐☐		$___	$___
Verbal Clarity	☐☐☐☐☐		$___	$___
Written Clarity	☐☐☐☐☐		$___	$___
Computer Skills:				
Application Use	☐☐☐☐☐		$___	$___
Computer Expert	☐☐☐☐☐		$___	$___
Specialized Skills:				
Advanced Degree	☐☐☐☐☐		$___	$___
Technical Sch.	☐☐☐☐☐		$___	$___
O-J-T Training	☐☐☐☐☐		$___	$___

Market Value Sub-Total $___ $___

Attitudinal:

Positive	☐☐☐☐☐	$___ $___
Outgoing	☐☐☐☐☐	$___ $___
Tenacious	☐☐☐☐☐	$___ $___

Multiply your total earnings by .5% for each category with a 4 or 5 rating in this section.

Total Market Value Range $___ $___
(Monthly Income X 12 for Annual Value)

Skills Market Value Chart & Worksheet

MIDDLE MANAGEMENT
Large Company ($500 Million +)
Large Metro Area (2 Million + Population)

Skills/Score

Management:	(Poor) 1 2 3 4 5 (Best)		Low	High
Administrative	☐☐☐☐☐		$____	$____
Delegation	☐☐☐☐☐		$____	$____
Financial	☐☐☐☐☐		$____	$____
Leadership	☐☐☐☐☐		$____	$____
Marketing	☐☐☐☐☐		$____	$____
Motivation	☐☐☐☐☐		$____	$____
Production	☐☐☐☐☐		$____	$____
Project Mgmt.	☐☐☐☐☐		$____	$____
Time Mgmt.	☐☐☐☐☐		$____	$____
Training Others	☐☐☐☐☐		$____	$____

Communication:

			Low	High
Listening	☐☐☐☐☐		$____	$____
Negotiation	☐☐☐☐☐		$____	$____
Persuasion	☐☐☐☐☐		$____	$____
Public Speaking	☐☐☐☐☐		$____	$____
Verbal Clarity	☐☐☐☐☐		$____	$____
Written Clarity	☐☐☐☐☐		$____	$____

Computer Skills:

			Low	High
Application Use	☐☐☐☐☐		$____	$____
Computer Expert	☐☐☐☐☐		$____	$____

Specialized Skills:

			Low	High
Advanced Degree	☐☐☐☐☐		$____	$____
Technical Sch.	☐☐☐☐☐		$____	$____
O-J-T Training	☐☐☐☐☐		$____	$____

Market Value Sub-Total $____ $____

Attitudinal:

			Low	High
Positive	☐☐☐☐☐	*Multiply your total earnings by .5% for each category with a 4 or 5 rating in this section.*	$____	$____
Outgoing	☐☐☐☐☐		$____	$____
Tenacious	☐☐☐☐☐		$____	$____

Total Market Value Range $____ $____
(Monthly Income X 12 for Annual Value)

Skills Market Value Chart & Worksheet

MIDDLE MANAGEMENT
Large Company ($500 Million +)
Medium City (250,000 — 2 Million Population)

Skills/Score

	(Poor) (Best) 1 2 3 4 5	100 200 300 400 500 600 700 800 900	Low	High
Management:				
Administrative	☐☐☐☐☐		$____	$____
Delegation	☐☐☐☐☐		$____	$____
Financial	☐☐☐☐☐		$____	$____
Leadership	☐☐☐☐☐		$____	$____
Marketing	☐☐☐☐☐		$____	$____
Motivation	☐☐☐☐☐		$____	$____
Production	☐☐☐☐☐		$____	$____
Project Mgmt.	☐☐☐☐☐		$____	$____
Time Mgmt.	☐☐☐☐☐		$____	$____
Training Others	☐☐☐☐☐		$____	$____
Communication:				
Listening	☐☐☐☐☐		$____	$____
Negotiation	☐☐☐☐☐		$____	$____
Persuasion	☐☐☐☐☐		$____	$____
Public Speaking	☐☐☐☐☐		$____	$____
Verbal Clarity	☐☐☐☐☐		$____	$____
Written Clarity	☐☐☐☐☐		$____	$____
Computer Skills:				
Application Use	☐☐☐☐☐		$____	$____
Computer Expert	☐☐☐☐☐		$____	$____
Specialized Skills:				
Advanced Degree	☐☐☐☐☐		$____	$____
Technical Sch.	☐☐☐☐☐		$____	$____
O-J-T Training	☐☐☐☐☐		$____	$____

Market Value Sub-Total $____ $____

Attitudinal:

	1 2 3 4 5		Low	High
Positive	☐☐☐☐☐	*Multiply your total earnings by .5% for*	$____	$____
Outgoing	☐☐☐☐☐	*each category with a 4 or 5 rating in*	$____	$____
Tenacious	☐☐☐☐☐	*this section.*	$____	$____

Total Market Value Range $____ $____
(Monthly Income X 12 for Annual Value)

Skills Market Value Chart & Worksheet
MIDDLE MANAGEMENT
Large Company ($500 Million +)
Small Metro Area (Less than 250,000 Population)

Skills/Score

	(Poor) (Best) 1 2 3 4 5	100 200 300 400 500 600 700 800 900	Low	High
Management:				
Administrative	☐☐☐☐☐		$___	$___
Delegation	☐☐☐☐☐		$___	$___
Financial	☐☐☐☐☐		$___	$___
Leadership	☐☐☐☐☐		$___	$___
Marketing	☐☐☐☐☐		$___	$___
Motivation	☐☐☐☐☐		$___	$___
Production	☐☐☐☐☐		$___	$___
Project Mgmt.	☐☐☐☐☐		$___	$___
Time Mgmt.	☐☐☐☐☐		$___	$___
Training Others	☐☐☐☐☐		$___	$___
Communication:				
Listening	☐☐☐☐☐		$___	$___
Negotiation	☐☐☐☐☐		$___	$___
Persuasion	☐☐☐☐☐		$___	$___
Public Speaking	☐☐☐☐☐		$___	$___
Verbal Clarity	☐☐☐☐☐		$___	$___
Written Clarity	☐☐☐☐☐		$___	$___
Computer Skills:				
Application Use	☐☐☐☐☐		$___	$___
Computer Expert	☐☐☐☐☐		$___	$___
Specialized Skills:				
Advanced Degree	☐☐☐☐☐		$___	$___
Technical Sch.	☐☐☐☐☐		$___	$___
O-J-T Training	☐☐☐☐☐		$___	$___

Market Value Sub-Total $___ $___

Attitudinal:

Positive	☐☐☐☐☐	*Multiply your total earnings by .5% for*	$___	$___
Outgoing	☐☐☐☐☐	*each category with a 4 or 5 rating in*	$___	$___
Tenacious	☐☐☐☐☐	*this section.*	$___	$___

Total Market Value Range $___ $___
(Monthly Income X 12 for Annual Value)

Skills Market Value Chart & Worksheet

MIDDLE MANAGEMENT
Medium Company ($50 Million — 500 Million)
Large Metro Area (2 Million + Population)

Skills/Score

	(Poor) (Best) 1 2 3 4 5		Low	High
Management:				
Administrative	☐☐☐☐☐		$____	$____
Delegation	☐☐☐☐☐		$____	$____
Financial	☐☐☐☐☐		$____	$____
Leadership	☐☐☐☐☐		$____	$____
Marketing	☐☐☐☐☐		$____	$____
Motivation	☐☐☐☐☐		$____	$____
Production	☐☐☐☐☐		$____	$____
Project Mgmt.	☐☐☐☐☐		$____	$____
Time Mgmt.	☐☐☐☐☐		$____	$____
Training Others	☐☐☐☐☐		$____	$____
Communication:				
Listening	☐☐☐☐☐		$____	$____
Negotiation	☐☐☐☐☐		$____	$____
Persuasion	☐☐☐☐☐		$____	$____
Public Speaking	☐☐☐☐☐		$____	$____
Verbal Clarity	☐☐☐☐☐		$____	$____
Written Clarity	☐☐☐☐☐		$____	$____
Computer Skills:				
Application Use	☐☐☐☐☐		$____	$____
Computer Expert	☐☐☐☐☐		$____	$____
Specialized Skills:				
Advanced Degree	☐☐☐☐☐		$____	$____
Technical Sch.	☐☐☐☐☐		$____	$____
O-J-T Training	☐☐☐☐☐		$____	$____

Market Value Sub-Total $____ $____

Attitudinal:

			Low	High
Positive	☐☐☐☐☐		$____	$____
Outgoing	☐☐☐☐☐	*Multiply your total earnings by .5% for each category with a 4 or 5 rating in this section.*	$____	$____
Tenacious	☐☐☐☐☐		$____	$____

Total Market Value Range $____ $____
(Monthly Income X 12 for Annual Value)

Skills Market Value Chart & Worksheet

MIDDLE MANAGEMENT
Medium Company ($50 Million — 500 Million)
Medium Metro Area (250,000 — 2 Million Population)

Skills/Score

	(Poor) (Best) 1 2 3 4 5		Low	High
Management:				
Administrative	☐☐☐☐☐		$____	$____
Delegation	☐☐☐☐☐		$____	$____
Financial	☐☐☐☐☐		$____	$____
Leadership	☐☐☐☐☐		$____	$____
Marketing	☐☐☐☐☐		$____	$____
Motivation	☐☐☐☐☐		$____	$____
Production	☐☐☐☐☐		$____	$____
Project Mgmt.	☐☐☐☐☐		$____	$____
Time Mgmt.	☐☐☐☐☐		$____	$____
Training Others	☐☐☐☐☐		$____	$____
Communication:				
Listening	☐☐☐☐☐		$____	$____
Negotiation	☐☐☐☐☐		$____	$____
Persuasion	☐☐☐☐☐		$____	$____
Public Speaking	☐☐☐☐☐		$____	$____
Verbal Clarity	☐☐☐☐☐		$____	$____
Written Clarity	☐☐☐☐☐		$____	$____
Computer Skills:				
Application Use	☐☐☐☐☐		$____	$____
Computer Expert	☐☐☐☐☐		$____	$____
Specialized Skills:				
Advanced Degree	☐☐☐☐☐		$____	$____
Technical Sch.	☐☐☐☐☐		$____	$____
O-J-T Training	☐☐☐☐☐		$____	$____

Market Value Sub-Total $____ $____

Attitudinal:

			Low	High
Positive	☐☐☐☐☐		$____	$____
Outgoing	☐☐☐☐☐	*Multiply your total earnings by .5% for each category with a 4 or 5 rating in this section.*	$____	$____
Tenacious	☐☐☐☐☐		$____	$____

Total Market Value Range $____ $____
(Monthly Income X 12 for Annual Value)

Skills Market Value Chart & Worksheet

MIDDLE MANAGEMENT
Medium Company ($50 Million — 500 Million)
Small Metro Area (Less than 250,000 Population)

Skills/Score

	(Poor) (Best) 1 2 3 4 5	100 200 300 400 500 600 700 800 900	Low	High
Management:				
Administrative	☐☐☐☐☐		$___	$___
Delegation	☐☐☐☐☐		$___	$___
Financial	☐☐☐☐☐		$___	$___
Leadership	☐☐☐☐☐		$___	$___
Marketing	☐☐☐☐☐		$___	$___
Motivation	☐☐☐☐☐		$___	$___
Production	☐☐☐☐☐		$___	$___
Project Mgmt.	☐☐☐☐☐		$___	$___
Time Mgmt.	☐☐☐☐☐		$___	$___
Training Others	☐☐☐☐☐		$___	$___
Communication:				
Listening	☐☐☐☐☐		$___	$___
Negotiation	☐☐☐☐☐		$___	$___
Persuasion	☐☐☐☐☐		$___	$___
Public Speaking	☐☐☐☐☐		$___	$___
Verbal Clarity	☐☐☐☐☐		$___	$___
Written Clarity	☐☐☐☐☐		$___	$___
Computer Skills:				
Application Use	☐☐☐☐☐		$___	$___
Computer Expert	☐☐☐☐☐		$___	$___
Specialized Skills:				
Advanced Degree	☐☐☐☐☐		$___	$___
Technical Sch.	☐☐☐☐☐		$___	$___
O-J-T Training	☐☐☐☐☐		$___	$___

Market Value Sub-Total $___ $___

Attitudinal:

			Low	High
Positive	☐☐☐☐☐	*Multiply your total earnings by .5% for*	$___	$___
Outgoing	☐☐☐☐☐	*each category with a 4 or 5 rating in*	$___	$___
Tenacious	☐☐☐☐☐	*this section.*	$___	$___

Total Market Value Range $___ $___
(Monthly Income X 12 for Annual Value)

Skills Market Value Chart & Worksheet
MIDDLE MANAGEMENT
Small Company (Less than $50 Million)
Large Metro Area (2 Million + Population)

Skills/Score

	(Poor) (Best) 1 2 3 4 5	100 200 300 400 500 600 700 800 900	Low	High
Management:				
Administrative	☐☐☐☐☐		$____	$____
Delegation	☐☐☐☐☐		$____	$____
Financial	☐☐☐☐☐		$____	$____
Leadership	☐☐☐☐☐		$____	$____
Marketing	☐☐☐☐☐		$____	$____
Motivation	☐☐☐☐☐		$____	$____
Production	☐☐☐☐☐		$____	$____
Project Mgmt.	☐☐☐☐☐		$____	$____
Time Mgmt.	☐☐☐☐☐		$____	$____
Training Others	☐☐☐☐☐		$____	$____
Communication:				
Listening	☐☐☐☐☐		$____	$____
Negotiation	☐☐☐☐☐		$____	$____
Persuasion	☐☐☐☐☐		$____	$____
Public Speaking	☐☐☐☐☐		$____	$____
Verbal Clarity	☐☐☐☐☐		$____	$____
Written Clarity	☐☐☐☐☐		$____	$____
Computer Skills:				
Application Use	☐☐☐☐☐		$____	$____
Computer Expert	☐☐☐☐☐		$____	$____
Specialized Skills:				
Advanced Degree	☐☐☐☐☐		$____	$____
Technical Sch.	☐☐☐☐☐		$____	$____
O-J-T Training	☐☐☐☐☐		$____	$____

Market Value Sub-Total $____ $____

Attitudinal:

			Low	High
Positive	☐☐☐☐☐	*Multiply your total earnings by .5% for each category with a 4 or 5 rating in this section.*	$____	$____
Outgoing	☐☐☐☐☐		$____	$____
Tenacious	☐☐☐☐☐		$____	$____

Total Market Value Range $____ $____
(Monthly Income X 12 for Annual Value)

Skills Market Value Chart & Worksheet
MIDDLE MANAGEMENT
Small Company (Less than $50 Million)
Medium Metro Area (250,000 — 2 Million Population)

Skills/Score

	(Poor) (Best) 1 2 3 4 5	100 200 300 400 500 600 700 800 900	Low	High
Management:				
Administrative	☐☐☐☐☐		$____	$____
Delegation	☐☐☐☐☐		$____	$____
Financial	☐☐☐☐☐		$____	$____
Leadership	☐☐☐☐☐		$____	$____
Marketing	☐☐☐☐☐		$____	$____
Motivation	☐☐☐☐☐		$____	$____
Production	☐☐☐☐☐		$____	$____
Project Mgmt.	☐☐☐☐☐		$____	$____
Time Mgmt.	☐☐☐☐☐		$____	$____
Training Others	☐☐☐☐☑		$____	$____
Communication:				
Listening	☐☐☐☐☐		$____	$____
Negotiation	☐☐☐☐☐		$____	$____
Persuasion	☐☐☐☐☐		$____	$____
Public Speaking	☐☐☐☐☐		$____	$____
Verbal Clarity	☐☐☐☐☐		$____	$____
Written Clarity	☐☐☐☐☐		$____	$____
Computer Skills:				
Application Use	☐☐☐☐☐		$____	$____
Computer Expert	☐☐☐☐☐		$____	$____
Specialized Skills:				
Advanced Degree	☐☐☐☐☐		$____	$____
Technical Sch.	☐☐☐☐☐		$____	$____
O-J-T Training	☐☐☐☐☐		$____	$____

Market Value Sub-Total $____ $____

Attitudinal:

	1 2 3 4 5		Low	High
Positive	☐☐☐☐☐	*Multiply your total earnings by .5% for each category with a 4 or 5 rating in this section.*	$____	$____
Outgoing	☐☐☐☐☐		$____	$____
Tenacious	☐☐☐☐☐		$____	$____

Total Market Value Range $____ $____
(Monthly Income X 12 for Annual Value)

Skills Market Value Chart & Worksheet

MIDDLE MANAGEMENT
Small Company (Less than $50 Million)
Small Metro Area (Less than 250,000 Population)

Skills/Score

	(Poor) (Best) 1 2 3 4 5		100 200 300 400 500 600 700 800 900	Low	High
Management:					
Administrative	☐☐☐☐☐			$____	$____
Delegation	☐☐☐☐☐			$____	$____
Financial	☐☐☐☐☐			$____	$____
Leadership	☐☐☐☐☐			$____	$____
Marketing	☐☐☐☐☐			$____	$____
Motivation	☐☐☐☐☐			$____	$____
Production	☐☐☐☐☐			$____	$____
Project Mgmt.	☐☐☐☐☐			$____	$____
Time Mgmt.	☐☐☐☐☐			$____	$____
Training Others	☐☐☐☐☐			$____	$____
Communication:					
Listening	☐☐☐☐☐			$____	$____
Negotiation	☐☐☐☐☐			$____	$____
Persuasion	☐☐☐☐☐			$____	$____
Public Speaking	☐☐☐☐☐			$____	$____
Verbal Clarity	☐☐☐☐☐			$____	$____
Written Clarity	☐☐☐☐☐			$____	$____
Computer Skills:					
Application Use	☐☐☐☐☐			$____	$____
Computer Expert	☐☐☐☐☐			$____	$____
Specialized Skills:					
Advanced Degree	☐☐☐☐☐			$____	$____
Technical Sch.	☐☐☐☐☐			$____	$____
O-J-T Training	☐☐☐☐☐			$____	$____

Market Value Sub-Total $____ $____

Attitudinal:

Positive	☐☐☐☐☐	$____ $____
Outgoing	☐☐☐☐☐	$____ $____
Tenacious	☐☐☐☐☐	$____ $____

Multiply your total earnings by .5% for each category with a 4 or 5 rating in this section.

Total Market Value Range $____ $____
(Monthly Income X 12 for Annual Value)

Skills Market Value Chart & Worksheet

FRONT LINE MANAGEMENT
Large Company ($500 Million +)
Large Metro Area (2 Million + Population)

Skills/Score

	(Poor) (Best) 1 2 3 4 5	100 200 300 400 500 600 700 800 900	Low	High
Management:				
Administrative	☐☐☐☐☐		$____	$____
Delegation	☐☐☐☐☐		$____	$____
Financial	☐☐☐☐☐		$____	$____
Leadership	☐☐☐☐☐		$____	$____
Marketing	☐☐☐☐☐		$____	$____
Motivation	☐☐☐☐☐		$____	$____
Production	☐☐☐☐☐		$____	$____
Project Mgmt.	☐☐☐☐☐		$____	$____
Time Mgmt.	☐☐☐☐☐		$____	$____
Training Others	☐☐☐☐☐		$____	$____
Communication:				
Listening	☐☐☐☐☐		$____	$____
Negotiation	☐☐☐☐☐		$____	$____
Persuasion	☐☐☐☐☐		$____	$____
Public Speaking	☐☐☐☐☐		$____	$____
Verbal Clarity	☐☐☐☐☐		$____	$____
Written Clarity	☐☐☐☐☐		$____	$____
Computer Skills:				
Application Use	☐☐☐☐☐		$____	$____
Computer Expert	☐☐☐☐☐		$____	$____
Specialized Skills:				
Advanced Degree	☐☐☐☐☐		$____	$____
Technical Sch.	☐☐☐☐☐		$____	$____
O-J-T Training	☐☐☐☐☐		$____	$____

Market Value Sub-Total $____ $____

Attitudinal:				
Positive	☐☐☐☐☐	*Multiply your total earnings by .5% for*	$____	$____
Outgoing	☐☐☐☐☐	*each category with a 4 or 5 rating in*	$____	$____
Tenacious	☐☐☐☐☐	*this section.*	$____	$____

Total Market Value Range $____ $____
(Monthly Income X 12 for Annual Value)

Skills Market Value Chart & Worksheet

FRONT LINE MANAGEMENT
Large Company ($500 Million +)
Medium Metro Area (250,000 — 2 Million Population)

Skills/Score

Management:	(Poor) 1 2 3 4 5 (Best)		Low	High
Administrative	☐☐☐☐☐		$___	$___
Delegation	☐☐☐☐☐		$___	$___
Financial	☐☐☐☐☐		$___	$___
Leadership	☐☐☐☐☐		$___	$___
Marketing	☐☐☐☐☐		$___	$___
Motivation	☐☐☐☐☐		$___	$___
Production	☐☐☐☐☐		$___	$___
Project Mgmt.	☐☐☐☐☐		$___	$___
Time Mgmt.	☐☐☐☐☐		$___	$___
Training Others	☐☐☐☐☐		$___	$___
Communication:				
Listening	☐☐☐☐☐		$___	$___
Negotiation	☐☐☐☐☐		$___	$___
Persuasion	☐☐☐☐☐		$___	$___
Public Speaking	☐☐☐☐☐		$___	$___
Verbal Clarity	☐☐☐☐☐		$___	$___
Written Clarity	☐☐☐☐☐		$___	$___
Computer Skills:				
Application Use	☐☐☐☐☐		$___	$___
Computer Expert	☐☐☐☐☐		$___	$___
Specialized Skills:				
Advanced Degree	☐☐☐☐☐		$___	$___
Technical Sch.	☐☐☐☐☐		$___	$___
O-J-T Training	☐☐☐☐☐		$___	$___

Market Value Sub-Total $___ $___

Attitudinal:

			Low	High
Positive	☐☐☐☐☐	*Multiply your total earnings by .5% for each category with a 4 or 5 rating in this section.*	$___	$___
Outgoing	☐☐☐☐☐		$___	$___
Tenacious	☐☐☐☐☐		$___	$___

Total Market Value Range $___ $___
(Monthly Income X 12 for Annual Value)

Skills Market Value Chart & Worksheet

FRONT LINE MANAGEMENT
Large Company ($500 Million +)
Small Metro Area (Less than 250,000 Population)

Skills/Score

Skills	(Poor) 1 2 3 4 5 (Best)	Low	High
Management:			
Administrative	☐☐☐☐☐	$____	$____
Delegation	☐☐☐☐☐	$____	$____
Financial	☐☐☐☐☐	$____	$____
Leadership	☐☐☐☐☐	$____	$____
Marketing	☐☐☐☐☐	$____	$____
Motivation	☐☐☐☐☐	$____	$____
Production	☐☐☐☐☐	$____	$____
Project Mgmt.	☐☐☐☐☐	$____	$____
Time Mgmt.	☐☐☐☐☐	$____	$____
Training Others	☐☐☐☐☐		
Communication:			
Listening	☐☐☐☐☐	$____	$____
Negotiation	☐☐☐☐☐	$____	$____
Persuasion	☐☐☐☐☐	$____	$____
Public Speaking	☐☐☐☐☐	$____	$____
Verbal Clarity	☐☐☐☐☐	$____	$____
Written Clarity	☐☐☐☐☐	$____	$____
Computer Skills:			
Application Use	☐☐☐☐☐	$____	$____
Computer Expert	☐☐☐☐☐	$____	$____
Specialized Skills:			
Advanced Degree	☐☐☐☐☐	$____	$____
Technical Sch.	☐☐☐☐☐	$____	$____
O-J-T Training	☐☐☐☐☐	$____	$____

Chart scale: 100 200 300 400 500 600 700 800 900

Market Value Sub-Total $____ $____

Attitudinal:

		Low	High
Positive	☐☐☐☐☐	$____	$____
Outgoing	☐☐☐☐☐	$____	$____
Tenacious	☐☐☐☐☐	$____	$____

Multiply your total earnings by .5% for each category with a 4 or 5 rating in this section.

Total Market Value Range $____ $____
(Monthly Income X 12 for Annual Value)

Skills Market Value Chart & Worksheet

FRONT LINE MANAGEMENT
Medium Company ($50 — $500 Million)
Large Metro Area (2 Million + Population)

Skills/Score

Skill	(Poor) 1 2 3 4 5 (Best)	Chart (100–900)	Low	High
Management:				
Administrative	☐☐☐☐☐		$___	$___
Delegation	☐☐☐☐☐		$___	$___
Financial	☐☐☐☐☐		$___	$___
Leadership	☐☐☐☐☐		$___	$___
Marketing	☐☐☐☐☐		$___	$___
Motivation	☐☐☐☐☐		$___	$___
Production	☐☐☐☐☐		$___	$___
Project Mgmt.	☐☐☐☐☐		$___	$___
Time Mgmt.	☐☐☐☐☐		$___	$___
Training Others	☐☐☐☐☐		$___	$___
Communication:				
Listening	☐☐☐☐☐		$___	$___
Negotiation	☐☐☐☐☐		$___	$___
Persuasion	☐☐☐☐☐		$___	$___
Public Speaking	☐☐☐☐☐		$___	$___
Verbal Clarity	☐☐☐☐☐		$___	$___
Written Clarity	☐☐☐☐☐		$___	$___
Computer Skills:				
Application Use	☐☐☐☐☐		$___	$___
Computer Expert	☐☐☐☐☐		$___	$___
Specialized Skills:				
Advanced Degree	☐☐☐☐☐		$___	$___
Technical Sch.	☐☐☐☐☐		$___	$___
O-J-T Training	☐☐☐☐☐		$___	$___

Market Value Sub-Total $___ $___

Attitudinal:

Skill	1 2 3 4 5	Low	High
Positive	☐☐☐☐☐	$___	$___
Outgoing	☐☐☐☐☐	$___	$___
Tenacious	☐☐☐☐☐	$___	$___

Multiply your total earnings by .5% for each category with a 4 or 5 rating in this section.

Total Market Value Range $___ $___
(Monthly Income X 12 for Annual Value)

Skills Market Value Chart & Worksheet

FRONT LINE MANAGEMENT
Medium Company ($50 — $500 Million)
Medium Metro Area (250,000 — 2 Million Population)

Skills/Score

	(Poor) (Best) 1 2 3 4 5	100 200 300 400 500 600 700 800 900		Low	High
Management:					
Administrative	☐☐☐☐☐			$____	$____
Delegation	☐☐☐☐☐			$____	$____
Financial	☐☐☐☐☐			$____	$____
Leadership	☐☐☐☐☐			$____	$____
Marketing	☐☐☐☐☐			$____	$____
Motivation	☐☐☐☐☐			$____	$____
Production	☐☐☐☐☐			$____	$____
Project Mgmt.	☐☐☐☐☐			$____	$____
Time Mgmt.	☐☐☐☐☐			$____	$____
Training Others	☐☐☐☐☐			$____	$____
Communication:					
Listening	☐☐☐☐☐			$____	$____
Negotiation	☐☐☐☐☐			$____	$____
Persuasion	☐☐☐☐☐			$____	$____
Public Speaking	☐☐☐☐☐			$____	$____
Verbal Clarity	☐☐☐☐☐			$____	$____
Written Clarity	☐☐☐☐☐			$____	$____
Computer Skills:					
Application Use	☐☐☐☐☐			$____	$____
Computer Expert	☐☐☐☐☐			$____	$____
Specialized Skills:					
Advanced Degree	☐☐☐☐☐			$____	$____
Technical Sch.	☐☐☐☐☐			$____	$____
O-J-T Training	☐☐☐☐☐			$____	$____

Market Value Sub-Total $____ $____

Attitudinal:

			Low	High
Positive	☐☐☐☐☐	*Multiply your total earnings by .5% for each category with a 4 or 5 rating in this section.*	$____	$____
Outgoing	☐☐☐☐☐		$____	$____
Tenacious	☐☐☐☐☐		$____	$____

Total Market Value Range $____ $____
(Monthly Income X 12 for Annual Value)

Skills Market Value Chart & Worksheet

FRONT LINE MANAGEMENT
Medium Company ($50 — $500 Million)
Small Metro Area (Less than 250,000 Population)

Skills/Score

Management:	(Poor) (Best) 1 2 3 4 5	Chart (100–900)	Low	High
Administrative	☐☐☐☐☐		$____	$____
Delegation	☐☐☐☐☐		$____	$____
Financial	☐☐☐☐☐		$____	$____
Leadership	☐☐☐☐☐		$____	$____
Marketing	☐☐☐☐☐		$____	$____
Motivation	☐☐☐☐☐		$____	$____
Production	☐☐☐☐☐		$____	$____
Project Mgmt.	☐☐☐☐☐		$____	$____
Time Mgmt.	☐☐☐☐☐		$____	$____
Training Others	☐☐☐☐☐		$____	$____

Communication:

	(Poor) (Best) 1 2 3 4 5		Low	High
Listening	☐☐☐☐☐		$____	$____
Negotiation	☐☐☐☐☐		$____	$____
Persuasion	☐☐☐☐☐		$____	$____
Public Speaking	☐☐☐☐☐		$____	$____
Verbal Clarity	☐☐☐☐☐		$____	$____
Written Clarity	☐☐☐☐☐		$____	$____

Computer Skills:

	(Poor) (Best) 1 2 3 4 5		Low	High
Application Use	☐☐☐☐☐		$____	$____
Computer Expert	☐☐☐☐☐		$____	$____

Specialized Skills:

	(Poor) (Best) 1 2 3 4 5		Low	High
Advanced Degree	☐☐☐☐☐		$____	$____
Technical Sch.	☐☐☐☐☐		$____	$____
O-J-T Training	☐☐☐☐☐		$____	$____

Market Value Sub-Total $____ $____

Attitudinal:

	(Poor) (Best) 1 2 3 4 5		Low	High
Positive	☐☐☐☐☐	*Multiply your total earnings by .5% for*	$____	$____
Outgoing	☐☐☐☐☐	*each category with a 4 or 5 rating in*	$____	$____
Tenacious	☐☐☐☐☐	*this section.*	$____	$____

Total Market Value Range $____ $____
(Monthly Income X 12 for Annual Value)

Skills Market Value Chart & Worksheet

FRONT LINE MANAGEMENT
Small Company (Less than $50 Million)
Large Metro Area (2 Million + Population)

Skills/Score

	(Poor) (Best) 1 2 3 4 5	100 200 300 400 500 600 700 800 900	Low	High
Management:				
Administrative	☐☐☐☐☐		$____	$____
Delegation	☐☐☐☐☐		$____	$____
Financial	☐☐☐☐☐		$____	$____
Leadership	☐☐☐☐☐		$____	$____
Marketing	☐☐☐☐☐		$____	$____
Motivation	☐☐☐☐☐		$____	$____
Production	☐☐☐☐☐		$____	$____
Project Mgmt.	☐☐☐☐☐		$____	$____
Time Mgmt.	☐☐☐☐☐		$____	$____
Training Others	☐☐☐☐☐		$____	$____
Communication:				
Listening	☐☐☐☐☐		$____	$____
Negotiation	☐☐☐☐☐		$____	$____
Persuasion	☐☐☐☐☐		$____	$____
Public Speaking	☐☐☐☐☐		$____	$____
Verbal Clarity	☐☐☐☐☐		$____	$____
Written Clarity	☐☐☐☐☐		$____	$____
Computer Skills:				
Application Use	☐☐☐☐☐		$____	$____
Computer Expert	☐☐☐☐☐		$____	$____
Specialized Skills:				
Advanced Degree	☐☐☐☐☐		$____	$____
Technical Sch.	☐☐☐☐☐		$____	$____
O-J-T Training	☐☐☐☐☐		$____	$____

Market Value Sub-Total $____ $____

Attitudinal:

			Low	High
Positive	☐☐☐☐☐	*Multiply your total earnings by .5% for each category with a 4 or 5 rating in this section.*	$____	$____
Outgoing	☐☐☐☐☐		$____	$____
Tenacious	☐☐☐☐☐		$____	$____

Total Market Value Range $____ $____
(Monthly Income X 12 for Annual Value)

Skills Market Value Chart & Worksheet

FRONT LINE MANAGEMENT
Small Company (Less than $50 Million)
Medium Metro Area (250,000 — 2 Million Population)

Skills/Score

Management: (Poor) 1 2 3 4 5 (Best)

	Low	High
Administrative	$___	$___
Delegation	$___	$___
Financial	$___	$___
Leadership	$___	$___
Marketing	$___	$___
Motivation	$___	$___
Production	$___	$___
Project Mgmt.	$___	$___
Time Mgmt.	$___	$___
Training Others	$___	$___

Communication:

	Low	High
Listening	$___	$___
Negotiation	$___	$___
Persuasion	$___	$___
Public Speaking	$___	$___
Verbal Clarity	$___	$___
Written Clarity	$___	$___

Computer Skills:

	Low	High
Application Use	$___	$___
Computer Expert	$___	$___

Specialized Skills:

	Low	High
Advanced Degree	$___	$___
Technical Sch.	$___	$___
O-J-T Training	$___	$___

Market Value Sub-Total $_____ $_____

Attitudinal:

		Low	High
Positive		$___	$___
Outgoing	*Multiply your total earnings by .5% for each category with a 4 or 5 rating in this section.*	$___	$___
Tenacious		$___	$___

Total Market Value Range $_____ $_____
(Monthly Income X 12 for Annual Value)

Skills Market Value Chart & Worksheet

FRONT LINE MANAGEMENT
Small Company (Less than $50 Million)
Small Metro Area (Less than 250,000 Population)

Skills/Score

Management: (Poor) 1 2 3 4 5 (Best)

- Administrative
- Delegation
- Financial
- Leadership
- Marketing
- Motivation
- Production
- Project Mgmt.
- Time Mgmt.
- Training Others

Communication:

- Listening
- Negotiation
- Persuasion
- Public Speaking
- Verbal Clarity
- Written Clarity

Computer Skills:

- Application Use
- Computer Expert

Specialized Skills:

- Advanced Degree
- Technical Sch.
- O-J-T Training

Scale: 100 200 300 400 500 600 700 800 900

Low High $_____ $_____ (for each skill row)

Market Value Sub-Total $_____ $_____

Attitudinal:

- Positive
- Outgoing
- Tenacious

Multiply your total earnings by .5% for each category with a 4 or 5 rating in this section.

$_____ $_____
$_____ $_____
$_____ $_____

Total Market Value Range $_____ $_____
(Monthly Income X 12 for Annual Value)

Chapter 7

Getting Help

YOU HAVE EVALUATED your skills and derived a dollar value for them. Now what? You are working six days a week and what time you have left is spent with the family or doing chores. How in the world do you find the time to look for another job? You have read all the self-help books you can lay your hands on, but you still need more advice and counseling to make your move. You need help. Relax! Help is available. Professional recruiting firms can save you time by doing some of the legwork. As for advice and counseling, there is a smorgasbord of options. Providing people with help to help themselves is big business.

How to Select the Right Help

Thousands of individuals and hundreds of organizations help people in their job search. It is a major industry involving consultants, corporations, colleges, universities, and churches with support groups. Many of these people and organizations have good intentions. Some of them are in it only to make money. Others are not qualified to be of real help to you. We will give you some guidelines for winnowing those that can help you from those that can't.

There are seven basic professional services available:

- Personal direction
- Career planning
- Resume writing
- Interview skills coaching
- Prospecting/marketing support
- Getting the job offer
- Ongoing moral support

It is worth spending time and money on professional help only if you really need it.

Personal Direction

Before spending any money, ask yourself, "Why do I need the help? Do I need more information, or am I trying to get someone else to make the decisions for me?"

Your mid-career crisis may be part of something larger, a mid-life crisis. This book does not deal with such a problem. You know if you are having more than a mid-career crisis from our definition of it in Chapter 1. If you are, you may need a substantial amount of help to boost your ability to cope with life. You may need a psychologist. Discuss this with your doctor or minister and ask them for a referral.

If you have only an old-fashioned career crisis and need more information, then seminars and support groups are low-cost ways to obtain it. Colleges, universities, and churches are places where such seminars can be found. The lowest cost of all is still your local library. You may just need to read the right books to help you find direction. A good one to start with is *Pathfinders* by Gail Sheehy.

Career Planning

Help with career planning can be found through counselors, consultants, and career planning companies. Most individual career counselors use self-assessment tools to help guide career direction. Career consultants are generally individuals with extensive business experience who, after an interview, will make suggestions about viable career options and people to contact. Career planning companies usually have group sessions where self-assessment and a high degree of interaction take place in order to facilitate learning about career opportunities.

The best way to find a good counselor or program for career planning is first to ask people you know. If you can't get a referral from them, call several counselors or organizations and ask for three client referrals. Interview each referral. Ask them why they chose the counselor or program. What did they like most? What help were they looking for? Did they get it? What did they like least? The answer to these questions should give you enough information to determine whether or not the counselor or program will meet your needs.

Ordinarily, a career planner will supply names of clients as references. If they don't, they will give you a preliminary interview to determine just how much help they can give you. Most organizations have a brochure that gives you detailed information about their program, or they have a person available who can answer questions.

Resume Writing

A good resume is always important in a job search, but for a mid-career changer it is even more important. Why? Because you have really great information to put in your resume: your years of experience, which, presented in the right manner, will make your career change possible.

Ask yourself what you want from this service. Do you want someone to help you determine what should go in the resume, or do you want someone who will help you improve the way the resume is written?

You may want help doing the entire resume. If you want someone to determine what should go in the resume, recognize that this will require a good deal of interview time and it will be necessary for the professional to understand what career you desire. As we will discuss in Chapter 11, a resume should be targeted for a specific career. If this is the type of professional you need, try to locate one through referral. Can't get a referral? Then contact several resume professionals and ask for client referrals whom you can interview. Ask these clients what made them select this professional. Did they get the service they were after?

You can get help with improving the wording of your resume through professional writing services. To evaluate a professional writing service, ask to look at some of the resumes it has prepared. Read them carefully and then ask yourself, "Would I interview the candidate presented in these resumes?" If you say yes after reading the resumes, then you have found a good service.

The telephone book and your local newspaper have listings and advertisements for professional resume services. Even printers advertise that they write and print resumes. *Remember, what you need is a resume that is an accurate reflection of your skills.*

Interview Skills Coaching

Because you are making a change in mid-career, it may be years since you have had an interview. There are even those lucky few out there who have had only one employment interview in their life! If the prospect of an interview makes you turn pale, your knees quake, and your mouth go dry, take it easy! There is support available for you.

However, this type of professional help is limited. Interviewing skills are probably among the most difficult to teach. What is really being taught are selling skills. Effective selling skills are acquired through much experience and a great deal of training, so don't expect too much from any training or coaching you find. If you do locate a class and have the time and resources to take it, sign up. It is bound to help. You will leave with at least one good idea to improve your interviewing skills, and that will make the training worthwhile.

Recruiters and placement agencies may have someone who can coach you. If not, they can put you in touch with a support group or consultant who can help you.

Chapter 12 will give you practical advice on how to deal with the crucial and sometimes intimidating interview.

Prospecting/Marketing Support

It has probably been years since you looked for a job. Not only that, your present job and other responsibilities leave you precious little time to find a new one. You may not know where to start, what is available, or what salary to expect. Recruiters and employment agencies can give you support.

A glance at the Yellow Pages of your telephone book will reveal dozens of recruiters and employment agencies waiting to help you find a job. They fall into two major groups, those who expect you to pay for their services and those who are employer paid.

Don't even consider using a service that expects you to pay for its help. Unless you lack *any* marketable skills, you should be able to either market yourself or use a recruiter or agency that is paid by the employer. If you have executive or technical skills, you can be listed with a recruiter or agency that specializes in such placements.

This topic is complex enough that we offer an entire section devoted to it. No matter what your qualifications are, or how limited your time may be, you do not want to depend solely upon a recruiter or agency to do your search. Employment agencies and recruiters fill only a small percentage of the jobs that are available on any given day. *Depending on the source you read, 75 percent to 85 percent of all jobs are filled through networking.*

We have a full discussion about networking in Chapter 10. To put it simply, networking is using your business contacts, family, and friends to help you make a career change. It is through business associates and friends at clubs or church that most jobs are found. Why do your business associates help you look for a job? Because there may come a time when they need the same help. A chief financial officer we know enlisted the help of his company's CPA and attorney in making a career change. Why would they help him? Because his move to another firm could possibly throw business their way.

Getting the Job Offer

Employment of any consequence usually requires more than one interview. Successfully filling a position is so important that very few companies rely on only one interview in making a decision. You may need help in securing follow-up interviews and in learning techniques to make you the outstanding candidate.

Many career coaches help with this step, and some of the career support organizations offer group sessions to analyze interview results. If you have not interviewed for a while, this type of support could be very valuable. What you need at this point are creative ideas to separate you from the other candidates. But don't spend a lot of money for them; we give you valuable pointers for getting the job offer in Chapter 12.

Ongoing Moral Support

The greatest help a career counseling organization can give you is moral support while you go through your mid-career crisis. As we have already discussed, it can be very demoralizing to make a mid-career change. It helps to know others are also finding it difficult and to exchange ideas about the best way to cope with the problems.

If you're not a joiner, then enlist the help of a friend who can meet with you on a regular basis. Get together for a weekly lunch or dinner. The purpose of your weekly meeting is to have your friend cheer you on your way. A friend who has been through the same problems also can give good advice.

The Power of a Professional Recruiter

There are four basic types of recruiters for you to choose from: the top ten retainer executive recruiters, smaller retainer executive recruiters, contingency recruiters, and placement agencies. Recruiters on retainer are paid by businesses to fill vacancies and to watch out for likely prospective employees. Contingency recruiters and placement agencies are paid for each vacancy they fill for a business.

The Top Ten

Some mid-career changers are in executive positions with enough responsibility and high enough pay to be attractive to the top group of executive recruiting firms, such as Korn/Ferry International or Paul R. Ray & Co., Inc. These firms are paid by corporations to find top-level executives. Getting the attention of one of these firms will do wonders for your career search, because they have access to companies and positions not available to you as an individual. You stand to get a higher salary through them than you could ever get on your own.

The challenge is getting their attention. In order to even be considered for inclusion in their database, your resume must show that you:

- earn $75,000 or more per year;
- have a college degree;
- work in a profession in demand; and
- have a good work history.

Earnings. Major retainer search firms recruit for jobs with annual starting salaries of $100,000 or more. They will consider individuals with exceptional credentials who earn $75,000 or more. They will justify to a prospective employer an income jump on the order of 33 percent for the right candidate.

College degree. When a company begins a search to replace one of its key executives, the minimum education required for a candidate is a bachelor's degree. Anyone without a degree is going to be difficult for a recruiter to sell. As a general rule, they don't bother to try. The more education, the better.

Profession in demand. Recruiters are in the business of selling products (people) to clients (businesses). They respond to market demand. Nuclear scientists may receive good salaries, but they are not a product in great demand. A nuclear scientist by training but a department manager by profession will have more opportunities. The industry in which you have worked is less important than the management skills you have acquired. You can always learn a new industry.

Five job groups are most in demand: general managers

(including CEO, president, division vice-president, and general manager); vice president of sales/marketing; vice president of finance (including treasurer and controller); vice president of human resources (including director of employee relations and director of labor relations); and vice president of information management systems (including director of management systems, director of manufacturing information systems, and director of data processing).

Good work history. Twelve jobs in twenty years is not a good work history. Twelve positions at the same company in twenty years is an excellent work history, provided the job changes reflect growth in skill and responsibility. Generally speaking, you should have at least two years' employment with your most recent employer. It is best if you have had five years with at least one employer.

Get in contact with one of the top ten recruiters if you meet the above criteria. They are listed in Appendix C of this book. Obtain the branch-office address and the name of the office manager for each city where you would like to work. Send a letter with a copy of your resume to each manager. Usually the large firms have one database to which all branch offices have access. However, you should send a letter to more than one office for several reasons. First, that office could have a search assignment for your specific area of expertise, so your resume would get immediate attention. Second, it is usually a researcher, rather than a placement recruiter, who decides whether or not your resume will be included in the database. One office may have standards slightly different from another's. Contacting each office as well as the headquarters could increase the chances of your resume being accepted.

Most of the firms do not consistently send notification of acceptance; it is your responsibility to find out. Call each office to which you sent a resume and ask for the researcher who handles the database. When you speak with the researcher, identify the person to whom you directed your letter and find out whether it has been received. If it has, ask whether you have been entered into the system. If you are not in the system, find out why you were not accepted.

After you have determined that your resume has passed the test and is in the database, your next challenge is to get an

interview. Ask how many searches are currently being conducted for people with your qualifications. You may find the
researcher will not be willing to talk openly with you. On the
other hand, the researcher may be very candid with you,
excluding the names of any clients, of course.

Retainer Recruiting Firms

The median income in 1988 for managers, executives, and
administrators was $37,000. That means that half earned more
than $37,000 and half earned less. Only a small percentage of
mid-career changers earn the kind of money that makes them
eligible for the top ten recruiters. There are many retainer
recruiting firms throughout the country that help people with
smaller annual earnings. All are listed in *The Directory of
Executive Recruiters,* available through your local library. It
lists firms and their addresses, along with the name of the
contact person for each firm. Call to verify any information
before sending a letter.

The directory indicates the starting salary for which each
firm conducts searches, so you can determine which firms will
be of help to you. Be sure to follow up with these firms just as
you would with the larger ones. Try to speak with the recruiter in each local firm to arrange an interview. They are always
looking for promising candidates.

Working with Contingency Recruiters

Contingency recruiters are busy. They have many searches in
progress because these firms are paid only for the vacancies
they fill. You may not obtain a preliminary face-to-face interview as a result. Still, you will almost always have an interview
before you are sent out to a prospective employer.

Placement Agencies

Placement agencies are found all over the country in all but
the smallest cities and towns. They differ from recruiters in
several ways. They are usually generalists. They have positions available in many different fields and at various income

and organizational levels. In the larger cities, there are agencies that specialize in one or two areas of employment. Data processing, clerical/secretarial, medical, and legal are some of the common specializations.

Some large agencies have branch offices, but most agencies are small and owner operated, an advantage for you if you are looking for a change but do not know what kind. Counselors in small agencies usually know the area well, and are familiar with the local as well as regional job market.

Today most of the positions these agencies are filling are fee paid, meaning the employer pays the agency a fee for finding the right employee. Just ten years ago most of the positions these agencies handled required the employee to pay the fee.

A Final Note

Professional help is available for any problems you may encounter while making your career change. Costs range from a few dollars for a library card to hundreds of dollars for a psychologist. Before seeking help, first decide the degree of assistance you need. If in doubt, start out by using the least costly source.

In the end, no matter what level of professional help you obtain, the results depend upon you. Professionals only give you guidance and leads. You must still do the follow-up and secure the job offer.

Chapter 8

Working for Yourself?

You now know that as a mid-career changer you possess knowledge and skills that have value in the workplace. These can be transferred to other careers. However, what does someone do if they have a good income in their present career, want out, but their skills and knowledge do not transfer successfully to another field? Or what if they can transfer to another field, but their true desire is for more challenge and independence? Establishing a business is one answer.

Much of what you know transfers to owning your own business as well as it does to working for someone else. This is particularly true of someone in a business managerial position. There are, however, major considerations in becoming an entrepreneur that do not exist when working for someone else.

The Seductive Lure of Owning Your Own Company

Statistics show that nine out of ten businesses fail within the first ten years. The main reason is too many people go into business without realizing the financial commitment and forty-eight–hour days required to make a success of it. This ignorance is the formula for disaster.

Both authors of this book have had personal experience with building a business, one a consulting practice and the other a franchise business. In addition, we have worked with several hundred individuals starting up their own businesses. We have learned a few things about what it takes to succeed.

The Essentials for Success

The skills and habits required to succeed as an entrepreneur are learned, but not everyone can learn them. Learning new habits takes time, which is something you won't have when starting a business.

Since you are in mid-career, you have acquired skills and developed personal characteristics that can be important to your success as a business owner. Listed below are fifteen skills and personal characteristics that we feel are essential for success in any type of business. How do your own skills and characteristics measure against these? List each one and rate your ability with either a 10 (high), 5 (moderate), or 0 (low). The ideal total score would be 150. If yours is less than 100, you might want to rethink your goal of becoming the world's newest tycoon.

1. A Vision

Every successful entrepreneur we have ever met had a vision. Inside themselves, deep down, successful business people believe they can make a difference, be the best, or lead the way. They *see* their destination. They light up when they talk about what they are doing. Money was never the number-one reason for starting the business. It may have been high on the list, but it was not number one. Neither was being their own boss. Again, it may have been high on the list, but it was not the first. *Number one was a vision of doing something, building something, or making something better.*

2. Persistence

A vision is not enough. You must also be willing to tough out the rough periods that come to every business. These include insufficient funds to meet payroll or other debts, the inability to meet production deadlines, problems with personnel, and just plain lack of business.

3. Ability to Handle Stress

Stress comes from a feeling that everything that can go wrong will: everyone wants delivery yesterday; the bank will loan you money only if you don't need it; federal, state, county, and city taxes and permits drain your cash; the competition is always one step ahead of you; and your employees won't show up on time.

You can do something about some of these things, but others are out of your hands. If you waste your time worrying about the things you cannot change, you will not have enough energy left to change the things you can.

4. Knowing How to Take Risks

A friend of ours says: "I never mind jumping into the pool—I just like to have my swimsuit on when I do." Successful entrepreneurs take risks, but they usually take measured risks. A measured risk is one that has been thoroughly assessed. The odds of the worst-case scenario have been examined and found acceptable; the decision is made to go ahead. Successful entrepreneurs take risks that many others would not take. They are more comfortable with risk than most people.

5. Seeing the Big Picture

You know the old saying "He can't see the forest for the trees." Too many people get so caught up with the details of everyday life that they cannot see what is going on around them. To be successful in business, you need to be able to take advantage of trends in your business or in the world around you. Depending upon the kind of business one owns, current events or political situations in this country or overseas can influence success or failure.

6. People Skills

Too many people want to become entrepreneurs because they are themselves difficult employees. They do not take orders or instructions well, thinking they know the right and only way something should be done. They usually are intolerant of anyone who holds different ideas or values. They do not get along with supervisors or coworkers. The answer, they think, is going into their own business.

Wrong! You can't get away from people. Your customers are people. Your employees are people. You must be able to motivate and maintain a good working relationship with employees. Equally important are the people skills you need to handle your customers. Without customers, you do not have a business. You must be able to attract and keep them through understanding, warmth, and sincerity.

7. Knowing Your Limits

A good understanding of your skills and strengths is essential for building a successful business. Too many entrepreneurs try to do everything in order to save money or have control. As a result, some things are done very poorly. As a mid-career changer you may have business skills, but you need to know your strengths and weaknesses. From this information, you can learn in what areas you need professional help (such as bookkeeping) and what characteristics you seek in employees.

8. Effective Networking

"Business is people," according to Mark McCormack on his audio tape *What They Don't Teach You at Harvard Business School.* He says that he learned the hard way that all business is based upon people and relationships. This is especially true when you are first starting out. It does not matter whether you are a cabinetmaker or a marketing consultant, the first work you get will most likely be due to relationships you have already established.

Even as your business grows, most of your best customers will be the result of networking relationships. You build up a network of business acquaintances before going into your own business, and you continue to develop and expand it as a business owner. Word-of-mouth referrals are the best way to build a business.

9. Hard Work

Some people go into business for themselves thinking they can work fewer hours or take time off at their whim. This is a big mistake in thinking! How can you possibly work less when you have everything you own—your house, cars, and all other major assets—mortgaged to the hilt to get the financing you need to go into business? With this kind of pressure, you work long hours during the day and worry about everything all night. We have never met a single successful business person who worked fewer hours during the first five years of building a business than they did for a former employer.

10. Good Listening

The 1980s were a decade in which corporate success was built upon effective marketing. During the 1960s and 1970s companies often succeeded because they built a better product or developed a product no one else had. For the most part, that competitive edge is gone. World competition has changed business; there are very few unique products and ideas to sell. Today business—even small business—has to be "marketing driven," regardless of the product or service.

How do you become marketing driven? By listening to your customers. Your market is the collective wants and desires of your current and prospective customers. Successful entrepreneurs talk to and *listen* to their customers.

11. Time Management

When you start your own business you will be doing the work of at least three people, but it will feel like twenty! If you are

doing the work of three people, you have to be efficient with
your time.

The single most important time management technique to
learn, if you have not already mastered it, is multiprocessing.
Multiprocessing is doing several tasks at one time. A practitioner of this concept recognizes that there is a difference
between the amount of actual time it takes to finish a task and
the amount of clock time required. For example, printing a
letter from a word processor may require three minutes of
clock time but only ten seconds of actual work time. The
remaining 170 seconds can be spent doing something else,
perhaps sorting expense receipts.

Multiprocessing is a must for the business owner. Don't
even *think* of starting your own business unless you have it
mastered.

12. Organization

To survive in business, you have to be well organized. Your
friendly government watchdogs require it, as do your customers. Employees become frustrated without it. If you run a
production business, you cannot deliver on time without it.
You cannot service customers well in a retail business with
employees unable to find anything.

13. Willingness or Ability to Work with Computers

It does not matter what business you are starting in today,
career counseling or horse training, you are going to have to be
computer literate. The minimum you will need to know is
word processing and record keeping. You cannot compete
without these aids.

Don't cringe and abandon all thought of going into business
because you know nothing about computers. There are wonderful word-processing packages available that require only a
matter of hours to master. The same is true of record-keeping
programs. The hardest step is walking into a computer store
and confessing to a man young enough to be your son that you

are a computer illiterate. Once you have done that, the rest is easy. We know from experience!

14. Solid Financial Knowledge

Banks know that the difference between a successful doctor and one whose practice fails is not their skills as physicians, but a knowledge of finance. The same is true of anyone who goes into business.

You can hire a professional to handle these matters, but you cannot depend upon that professional to do everything for you. You must be aware of your tax responsibilities. You must be knowledgeable about cash flow. You must have a handle on inventory management. You need to have enough knowledge and information to make competent decisions regarding the allocation and investment of your money.

15. Creativity

Equal to marketing awareness, creativity is the most talked-about skill requirement for entrepreneurs. You need to be creative in business because your competition is, and because your customers demand it. You always have to be looking for new ways to build, package, or sell your products and services. Customers like something new and different. It takes creativity to remain fresh and to stay ahead of your competition.

Creativity is learnable. It simply requires looking at the world differently from how you do now. Creativity guru Mike Vance, who worked with Walt Disney for years, says: "Creativity is the making of the new and the rearranging of the old in a new way."

You may not think of yourself as creative. Perhaps you have not given yourself credit for the creativity you have. How many times have you looked at something and said, "Wouldn't this be better if they had just made it like this?" or "Wouldn't this be better if they had added that to it?" Thinking of improvements with "this" change or "that" addition is creativity—"rearranging of the old in a new way."

Where Should You Start?

So you have scored over 100 on the essential skills and personal characteristics list. Now you are hot to trot after your own business. How should you go into business? Should you start your own, or should you buy an existing business? As a mid-career changer, you have an advantage over a young person starting out in the business world. You are at a point in life when you have accumulated assets that can be turned into cash. This cash will allow you to buy a business that is already started, or to buy a franchise where you can get the help and advice you need for success.

Franchises

Franchising is big business. Mid-career changers are favorite targets for two reasons: 1) the fact that they are considering making a change means they are willing to take a risk; 2) they have money. It costs as much (and sometimes more) to buy some of the more successful franchises as it does to start a business from the ground up or to buy an existing successful business.

The franchise business makes many claims about improving the odds for success and about eliminating many of the headaches associated with establishing a business. Some of the claims are true, some are not.

For example, a franchisor may say that none of their locations has ever failed. The franchisor can mask the number of business failures by assisting in selling a location that is in trouble. The new owner brings additional cash into the business, prolonging its life or even making it a success. By selling the business, often at a loss to the owner, the location does not go down as a failure.

Promises about training, support, and advertising are often much greater than what is delivered. For this reason, many franchisees soon begin to resent the 6 to 9 percent of gross sales they have to send the parent company every month.

If you are considering a franchise, investigate the organization carefully. Remember the franchisor has a vested interest in keeping each location open, not necessarily in making you a success. Each time the franchise location is sold, the franchisor usually gets a piece of the action. If you investigate carefully, you will see that some franchise companies make the majority of their money from opening new locations and selling existing stores, rather than from the revenue generated by product sales.

Successful franchises require a substantial investment and as much commitment as starting a business independently. A franchisee can expect advice and advertising campaigns from the franchisor, and also the help and support of other franchise owners.

If you are considering a particular franchise, be sure you check it out with the current owner. Have a lawyer look over the contract before you sign it; he is the only one who can spot language that may cause you problems later. If the franchisor cannot answer your attorney's questions satisfactorily, do not sign.

If the franchise deal looks too good to be true, it probably is.

Buying an Existing Business

As with a franchise, buying an existing business may eliminate many of the problems a new business will entail. Still, you must consider the following when evaluating the purchase of any business: debt service, cash flow, inventory, existing customer base, and potential growth/expansion. Know what you are getting before you write out a check. Talk to the owner and consult with his accountant. If you are uncomfortable after these discussions, engage a specialist. It will be worth the money.

With interest rates in the double digits, debt service is no small matter today for the average business. An existing company that earns $75,000 in profit before taxes may sell for $350,000 or more, depending upon location and market conditions. Servicing a debt of up to $350,000 (you will have to pay some portion of the price as a down payment) could cost you over $50,000 per year in principle and interest payments. With that payment now included in your overhead, that

$75,000 is earning you only $25,000 per year. The owner may tell you that he has not raised prices in two years and that you can raise them and thereby generate an immediate 10 percent increase in revenue, eliminating the debt service problem. Beware! He probably has not raised prices because he has price-sensitive customers and lots of competition. Otherwise, why would he be letting that much profit walk out the door?

Debt service influences profit margins and also cash flow. Cash flow, however, is also affected by other business factors. What are the receivables like? How old are they? How many customers are there? How wide is the customer base? Are there lots of customers, or do one or two large ones generate most of the sales volume? If the latter, what is the credit risk with those few customers? What would happen to the business if those large customers were lost? What are vendor relations like? How much credit can you get from them? What will they do with a new owner? Will they raise the price on your supplies?

Inventory is a great place to get into trouble. The owner may tell you that you are buying $50,000 worth of finished goods or raw materials. Be careful. It may be $45,000 worth of boat anchors and only $5,000 worth of boats. Be sure you understand how much inventory turnover the owner has had each year, and research how that stacks up to an industry average. Inventory can be a cash hog or a cash cow.

The existing steady customers are your bread and butter. Will they stay with you if you buy the business? It may be difficult to evaluate, but you must try to get a feel for it. What percentage are they of the receivables? If a change causes you to lose even 20 percent of your existing customer base, you may find yourself losing so much money that you cannot generate enough new sales before it is too late.

Finally, what is the realistic opportunity for growth? How many competitors are there and what are they doing to gain market share? Is the market large enough to let you grow? Is the market growing, too? Is the opportunity for growth that the seller presents valid when compared to his track record?

When you purchase a company, it cannot stay the same size. It is immediately supporting two families—the previous owner's (with your monthly payments) and yours. Give serious consideration to this fact before you buy.

Starting Your Own Business

It takes a lot of courage to give up a regular paycheck and go into business for yourself, and a franchise or existing business can lessen the risk. But you may have an original idea, or there may not be an existing business or franchise that interests you, so you start a business from the ground up.

The first thing you will need is money. Hat in hand, you pay a visit to your friendly banker. He will tell you that you may be brilliant in your career and have a great idea for a business, but without previous experience he cannot lend you any money. He can, however, lend you money by your mortgaging your house, cars, real estate, your first child, and your favorite pet. In other words, without prior business experience you cannot get a business loan. Instead, everything of value that you own will have to be used to raise the money. This is what gives you the incentive to make a success of the business!

Before you make the commitment, know the three circumstances you will face as a beginning entrepreneur.

First, you probably will not earn a profit from the business for the first two years. However, sometime within that period the business should generate enough revenue for you to begin drawing a salary that covers your living expenses. If the business actually earns a profit in those first two years, it is an exception.

Second, expect to invest twice as much as you figure in your original business plan. It's like moving into a new house: you never anticipate all of the cash drains that arise in a new business.

Third, your original marketing plan will probably be off the mark and you will find the market different from your expectations once you are actually working in it. Do not spend a lot of money on fancy brochures too early in your business development. You will have more urgent uses for that cash, and the brochures will be outdated and unusable within six months.

Develop something simple in the beginning and save your money until you know exactly what four-color pieces you will need.

These three considerations may sound crazy to you now, but ask ten entrepreneurs who have been in business for five years or less about each one, and you will find nine out of the ten will admit that they encountered all of those problems.

If you have enough money to live for two years without income from the business, and you have an exciting idea you would like to build into a business, go for it. It's harder than you ever dreamed, but worth it if you succeed. Appendix B of this book is a resource list that can provide you with further information.

Building a Company or Shaping a Practice

There is a difference between a business and a practice. As a mid-career changer, you probably have the means and the experience to go in either direction.

Fundamentally, a practice is based upon the reputation of an individual, such as a management consultant or a doctor. A business is based upon the reputation of a company name and location, such as Bloomingdale's. A practice is usually a personal service delivered by a professional. A business is usually a product or service delivered by a number of people. A practice usually involves promoting the reputation of the main practitioner. A business usually involves promoting the value of the product or service. A practice has to be passed on to another owner carefully, presenting constancy to its clients. A business can generally be sold without disturbing much of the customer base.

If you want to build a practice, you must look at how promotable *you* are as an individual. You must be, or become, an effective public speaker. You will need to gain visibility in your community. Making presentations about your specialty to groups of professionals and business people is the most effective tool you have to promote your practice.

In building a business, you will focus attention on your

product or service. You want *it* to become your star attraction. Look for creative ways to get attention for the product.

If you want to build a practice, you can use your name in the company name. If you want to build a business that can be sold, give your company a name that represents the product or service the business delivers. It is much more difficult to sell a business that has the founder's name on it. A large part of a company's equity is in its name and reputation. With the founder's name as the name of the business, a portion of that equity could be lost in a sale that resulted in a name change.

Finally, a practice is often easier to build than to sell. What are your long-term goals? If you want to develop a business that you can still be working when you are eighty-five, consider a practice. If you want to sell out in five years for $5 million, you are going to have to build a business.

On Your Own or Work for Others?

Before starting out on your own, evaluate where you stand on our list of essential skills and personal characteristics. Did you score at least 100? If not, are you sure you have the right skills and characteristics to go into business for yourself?

You may have the vision and the desire, but do you want to take the risk? Do you feel confident enough to go into business knowing that if you fail, you may lose some or all of the assets you have accumulated? Where do you want to start? Should you buy a franchise, buy an existing business, or build a practice?

If you have the vision, know where you are going to start, and want to take the risk, you are indeed a person with the kind of courage and spirit of adventure it takes to go into business for yourself.

If going into business is not your cup of tea, then you will be interested in the next chapter, which discusses the advantages and disadvantages of working in the public and private sectors, as well as in large and small businesses.

Chapter 9

Where Do You Fit: Public, Private, Large, or Small?

MOST PEOPLE ARRIVE at mid-career after working fifteen to twenty years in one sector of the economy. There are two major sectors that make up our system: public (all governments) and private. For our purpose, we break down the private sector further into corporate giants and small businesses. Each has a distinct milieu. Workers in one sector often know little about another sector and often disdain the people who work in it. Many private-sector employees feel that all government workers are overpaid and underworked. People who work for small businesses feel the same way toward employees of large corporations.

By definition, as a mid-career changer you are looking for choices. How can you make an intelligent choice if you know nothing about the other options?

This chapter will give you a yardstick to help evaluate the

advantages and disadvantages of employment in both the public and private sectors and large and small businesses. Our research included interviews with dozens of federal, state, county, and city government employees as well as employees from large and small companies.

The Pros and Cons of the Public and Private Sectors

For the purpose of comparing differences between the public and private sectors, we asked employees to rate their employers in six important areas:

1. Employment opportunities for outsiders
2. Rate of pay
3. Growth/promotion opportunities
4. Moving/relocation
5. Child care
6. Insurance and retirement benefits

Employment Opportunities for Outsiders

Government. Without prior federal government or military experience, it is very difficult to secure a job working for the federal government today unless you are willing to start at the bottom. A federal government personnel administrator told us that every posted job has from ten to one hundred outside applicants. Most federal and state agencies try to promote from within; thus entry-level positions are at the bottom. Mid-career moves from public to private are done more often than the other way around. Counties and cities are more open to outsiders at higher levels than are the federal and state governments.

To become eligible for a job at any level of government you must test for that job classification. If your score is high enough, you will then be put on an eligibility list. It is this list that is reviewed by hiring managers at the time of an opening.

Private Sector. There are more employment opportunities in the private sector, but there can also be a degree of discrimination against former public employees. Some people feel public employees do not know how to work as hard as those in private business. These people feel that public employees have not had to answer to the bottom line, so they do not have the same outlook on fiscal management as employees in the private sector. If that was ever true, it is certainly undergoing a change today with the belt-tightening at all levels of government.

Some large corporations prefer to promote from within. The only way to enter the work force of such a company is to start at a low-level position. Such corporations believe this is necessary to protect career opportunities for current employees. Some companies do this to protect corporate culture. They believe the way they conduct business can be learned only by working one's way up the corporate ladder.

The only way to enter such a company on a management level is to find a manager who believes *you* are the only person who can do the job they have open. Your uniqueness then overcomes the "promote from within" philosophy.

Rate of Pay

Pay and fringe benefits are of more concern to you in mid-career than when you were starting out. You now have a family to support and other obligations. Child and health care benefits are much more important to you now. In fact, a lack of these may be one reason you want to make a change.

Government. Federal, state, and local government pay has traditionally been lower than pay in the private sector. This is not true in geographic areas where government has to compete in a tight labor market to attract employees, or for certain hard-to-fill job classifications. In very small or poor communities, federal and state pay may be much higher than that of private business in the area. The federal government uses the nation as a whole to figure rates of pay. State governments review the salaries of neighboring states to set pay scales. If a local economy is small or depressed, such government jobs will have relatively higher wages. The reverse is also true. If the local economy is very robust, government pay may be behind. This is especially true if there is low turnover in government jobs. Under those circumstances there is no need to adjust the pay scale to compete.

Private Sector. By studying the pay grids in Chapter 6, you know that private-sector pay varies by size of city, size of company, and level of management. However, there are always exceptions. As a general rule, a small privately held company will not pay as much as a large public company. Geography is an influence on the rate of pay. A company in Los Angeles, California, will have to pay a worker more than a company in De Ridder, Louisiana, will.

Most private employers have more flexibility than government to pay well for the qualified personnel they feel they really need. Pay is generally spoken of in terms of ranges. Never forget that an exceptionally desirable prospective employee can negotiate pay. A pay range can be extended or a job reclassified. If this becomes the situation for you during a change, be sure you address the issue of future promotions and raises *before* you accept the job. As soon as you have accepted the job you have lost your power to negotiate.

Growth/Promotion Opportunities

Government. Many of our government interviewees felt their jobs offered them an opportunity to "do good," or that they were truly "serving the people." They felt such positions are not available in private business.

Others believed the private sector offers to an outstanding person more rewards and recognition than government does. They felt there is more opportunity for faster advancement in the private sector.

Government managers at mid-level and higher whom we interviewed felt their jobs to be more secure than their counterparts in private industry. They believed that the government takes a long-term view of management skills, measuring a manager based on his leadership and motivation rather than against the bottom line only.

It is a common belief that government service is an ideal training ground to prepare for a second career in private business. This belief is reinforced by a general consensus among the people we interviewed that a government career should be your first career, not your second.

For years there was discrimination against women and minorities. Today the reverse seems to be true. One city personnel employee we interviewed told us that every job opening generates two lists: one that lists the top five eligible candidates, and a second list that ranks the top five eligible women and minority candidates. The hiring manager is encouraged to work from the second list.

Private Sector. Large companies are very aware of the important role they have in helping women and minorities move ahead. However, they do not appear to be practicing reverse discrimination to the same degree as government—unless the employer is doing a great deal of government work and has to meet government employment goals.

Our research shows that many white males age thirty or older feel that because of reverse discrimination the best career opportunities are found in self-employment or working for small companies.

Smaller companies are dominated by white males at the top and women at the bottom. Promotions past supervisor are still difficult for women unless they are exceptional or find an exceptional company. There is a general feeling that this is changing, though it is hard to find statistics to back it up.

Moving/Relocation

Government. The federal government has become much more sensitive to the concept of *family* relocation. It is aware that 70 percent of all households have two incomes. The federal government will usually help the spouse of the transferring employee find employment.

Most families who move for the government find the people at the new office very helpful. Anyone who has worked for the federal government for five years or more has probably moved to secure a promotion. Veteran employees understand what it feels like to arrive at a new town, a new house, and a new job. They are willing to help fellow employees make the adjustment.

Private Sector. During the 1960s and 1970s people who worked for IBM said that the company's initials stood for "I've Been Moved." If during your job interview with IBM you said you were not willing to relocate, you were not hired. Many other large companies had the same attitude.

Things have improved. Relocation is still important for career growth in most large companies, but generally, refusing to move will not end your career as it once would. Korn/Ferry International's 1989 senior executive survey reported the average senior executive had relocated three times during his career. Nineteen percent of the respondents said they had refused to relocate. Eighty-seven percent of those said they did not feel the refusal had adversely affected their careers.

Child Care

Government. According to the U.S. Bureau of Labor Statistics, women are now 44 percent of the work force. This, plus the fact that in 70 percent of all households both adults work, means child care has become a major concern for both employee and employer. Child care problems account for up to eight missed workdays per year for the responsible adult. Child care is ranked as the second most-wanted employee benefit, and many government employers have evolved effective solutions.

Child care varies from one agency to another in the federal government. Some agencies offer nothing, and some offer exceptional care facilities within the same building as the working parent. One of our interview respondents commented that she felt her agency's child care facility had an excellent staff. But what she appreciates most is the fact that the facility keeps the same working hours she does. She has friends working in the private sector who are not as fortunate. They have problems with their child care providers when they have to work late or come in early.

Though large typing pools are a thing of the past in government offices, it is mostly women who run the computers. A plurality of government employees are working women with children. As a result, government employers are aware of the problems of the working mother. If they do not offer a child care facility, they will at least be understanding of the added burden created by being a working mother.

Private Sector. Private business is beginning to recognize the need to reduce the stress caused by child care problems. A 1989 poll taken by *The New York Times* found that 36 percent of employed mothers work to support their families. That is, they are not working because they want to, they are working because they have to. According to a November 20, 1989, article in *Industry Week*, 11 percent of U.S. employers are offering child care assistance. That same article said, ". . . by 1995, workplace [child care] centers will be commonplace at [large] companies." The tight labor markets predicted for the 1990s may rouse more companies to offer child care benefits as part of their strategy for recruiting and retaining employees.

Child care is not just a women's issue. In a 1988 *Inc.* magazine article, a survey of working parents with children under two years of age found that 89 percent of the women and 62 percent of the men experienced work-related child care problems.

If child care is an important part of your mid-career change, do not hesitate to ask any prospective employer about the company program. Today it will not be a poor reflection upon you, nor should it cause an employer to wonder if you are going to be a problem employee. Instead, the employer should be aware of the need and should be answering it.

Insurance and Retirement Benefits

Government. Federal, state, and most local governments participate in retirement programs that are coordinated with Social Security. The federal government is no longer outside the Social Security system. One of the major reasons for this change was to infuse more money into the system. Most retirement programs for public employees are excellent. The programs vary from offering early retirement options after twenty years at 50 percent of your last year's pay, to retirement at sixty-five with 50 percent or more of the average of your last five years' pay.

Medical insurance for public employees ranges from adequate to excellent. Usually, the larger the employer, the better the coverage. Most of the time there is a choice of insurers and programs so that each employee has some say in how much he pays for insurance. Dental and eye care coverage are common.

Private Sector. Very few companies offer retirement programs equal to those offered during the 1960s by companies such as Sears, Roebuck and Company. Years ago Sears offered a matching-funds program of one dollar for every one dollar an employee put away into his retirement program.

Today, 401(k) plans may offer some small matching funds, but we could not find a single company that matched the old Sears program. The spree of mergers and buyouts in the late seventies and in the eighties greatly affected retirement programs. Many buyouts were initiated simply for the pool of cash sitting in employee retirement funds.

Medical insurance plans vary greatly from company to company. Some companies have little coverage with high deductibles, and others will include everything. The amount contributed by the employee also will vary. Do not assume anything when interviewing. The cost of medical insurance has become so great for employers that they are looking for ways to control or reduce it. You may find that you will have reduced initial coverage when you change jobs or careers. Before you accept a job, talk to the human resources person if necessary, and get a clear understanding of just what is covered by the medical plan and what you are expected to contribute toward it.

Advantages and Disadvantages of Big Companies vs. Small

A mid-career changer who has worked for government or a large corporation has worked in a completely different environment from that of someone who has spent his working life in small business. We will highlight some of the major differences between them so you can judge for yourself if the solution to your mid-career crisis should include a move from one to the other.

Advantages of Working for a Giant

A company the size of IBM has many advantages. For example, if you are in finance at IBM, you have access to the top CPAs in the country. If you need legal advice, you have lawyers on staff who can help. If you want to go to Disneyland, you can get employee discount coupons.

Large companies have a greater degree of security than do small companies. Size gives you a chance to move within the company. Many times when you read about a large layoff planned for a giant company, the newspapers print only half the story. The company may plan a reduction of three thousand employees, but most of those employees have the chance to find jobs in other divisions. One of our client companies had a layoff of two thousand employees that resulted in only five hundred people actually losing their jobs. That's not to say that five hundred people isn't a lot, but three-fourths of those originally laid off found jobs within the company's other divisions.

Giants offer career growth and income that cannot be matched by small companies. In his book *The Success Profile*, Lester Korn said the average compensation, in 1987 dollars, for senior executives of large retail corporations was $265,000. Industrial companies paid an average of $247,000. Very few small companies can give their executives that kind of compensation.

The time and dollars put into the training programs of many large companies are unmatched anywhere. If you want to change careers and get on-the-job training, the best available is through some of the large corporations. IBM, Xerox, and Hewlett-Packard offer some of the best sales training found in the United States. Bank of America is the Harvard for bankers. General Electric can turn you into the best technical services representative in the country. Moore Business Forms can train you to be an expert in forms design and sales. Small companies cannot afford to put an employee through six months or a year of training during which time they receive little or no return on work performed. Large companies feel they cannot afford *not* to train employees to meet a high standard of excellence.

Large companies generally offer a greater opportunity to travel and relocate to other parts of the country or even outside the United States. Small firms do not have the multiple divisions and branch offices which make such moves possible.

Finally, large companies almost always offer the best benefits package. Size gives them the power to negotiate good deals for themselves and their employees. A large employee pool means that the cost of benefits is shared by more people.

Advantages of Working for a Smaller Company

Jon is an example of the difference between a large and a small company employee. He is the chief financial officer for a $35-million-a-year company. His prior position was a division controller for a $5 billion company. He feels his greatest advantage in working for a smaller company is his ability to make decisions. There is less bureaucracy and fewer managers, and each one has more responsibility. There is greater risk, too. If he decides to make an equipment investment of several million dollars and the equipment does not work out well, he could put his company into a tough financial position. If it works out well, he has the reward of knowing *his* decision made a difference. At his old company, he would not have had the chance to make the decision at all.

A number of the managers we interviewed thought a smaller company offers the opportunity to see how all parts of the business—finance, sales, engineering—interrelate. You get to really learn what makes a business tick.

Small companies offer flexibility. Often a new problem or situation means new solutions need to be found. There will not be a policy to cover it. Instead, the employee gets the challenge to create a solution.

A small company may be your ticket to financial independence. Many of them have given stock options to employees starting out with the company, making the employees millionaires when it grew into a big-time corporation.

Disadvantages of Giants

"When you're riding an elephant, you don't worry about the ants," a corporate chief once said about his company. While this is true, it is also impossible to change the direction of a charging elephant.

Big companies are usually *very* slow to act. It can take years to get a new idea accepted. Spin-off companies are often created by someone who developed a product idea at a large corporation only to have them sit on it.

Big companies can be too layered with management. You can find yourself ten layers removed from the president, thus being in the dark about the strategy and direction of the company.

Finally, large companies can be too structured. They don't like to be told this, but many of them operate the same as a government bureaucracy. Many companies have policy manuals that cover everything from how to hire an employee to how to change a light bulb. Too many people in the company become obsessed with doing everything by the book. This makes for a company that is entrenched and lacks creativity and spontaneity. In some cases, this actually leads to a loss of market share.

Disadvantages of a Small Company

Lack of support is the most common complaint with small companies. Resources cost money and small companies need to make every penny count. Small companies buy paper by the box instead of by the case. Legal advice for a small company comes from an attorney on retainer, rather than from its own legal department. Small companies start a new department by asking someone to "spend a few hours a week taking care of this."

Small companies can impede the growth of your career. There is usually little room at the top of the ladder. Advancement often means moving to a larger firm with more opportunities and higher income potential.

In Summary

In this chapter we have discussed the differences between working for the public and private sectors of the economy and between large and small businesses.

Keep several points in mind when making a decision to move from one to the other. Large public employers and large companies have many similarities. As a rule, the many departments, divisions, field offices, and general diversity required of a large employer mean more opportunities for career advancement within the organization.

But many people feel that the stability offered by such bureaucracy also stifles the individual. These people prefer smaller employers where the individual can make a difference in the success or failure of the business.

Each of these areas—public agency, private sector, large corporation, small company—has definite advantages and disadvantages. When making your decision, keep in mind what you *really* want out of your mid-career change. You have spent years working in one of these areas. What type of working environment do you think you will enjoy the most?

After reading the first nine chapters of this book, you should now know:

1. the definition of mid-career syndrome;
2. how to measure the security of your present job;
3. about your own personal values;
4. that you have many skills;
5. that your skills are transferable;
6. how to measure the value of your skills;
7. where to get help if you need it;
8. the advantages and disadvantages of working for yourself and for someone else; and
9. the advantages and disadvantages of working for government, large corporations, and small businesses.

The next three chapters are devoted to the mechanics of making a mid-career change. You now know where you want your mid-career change to take you; we will show you how to get there.

Chapter 10

How to Market Yourself

YOU PROBABLY never thought of yourself as a product, but in your career, *you* are the product. Your work history, education, training, personality, appearance, desires, and goals make up a unique product—you. In the world of business, products are sold by promotion; to promote a product, a marketing plan is required.

What is a marketing plan? A marketing plan identifies and defines the product. It also profiles the product's market and defines its position in the marketplace. The product is then packaged to reflect its best image. Finally, it is aggressively promoted and then sold. You must take these same steps to successfully make your career change.

You might think having a job hinders your mid-career change because you cannot devote enough time to it. Not true. It is true that the search may take longer, but that does not outweigh the benefits of keeping your current job. There are several ways to make time for interviews and telephone work. You can change your lunch hour to an earlier or later time, or you might be able to change a day off to one during the week. You could change your working hours to have time in the morning or afternoon for your search. Many employers will not object to your making a career change as long as it does not interfere with your work. If such is the case, your boss will work with you to make time available. In other instances, if you're in sales, for example, you will have to work covertly. Many prospective employers will schedule interviews around your working hours. Direct mail, networking, and private placement agencies can all be managed to aid the search of anyone currently employed. Remember, employers prefer to hire someone who is employed—working people change jobs every day.

Chapter 12 will help you deal with the objections you encounter during interviews if you are currently out of work. Give serious consideration to finding a temporary position or working for a temporary agency in order to have a job while you search.

Keep an old Chinese saying in mind during your career-change marketing campaign: "A pound of pluck is worth a ton of luck." As we discussed in Chapter 5, it takes effort, time, and money to make a successful change. The greater the change, the more required from you.

Developing Your Marketing Plan

Your marketing plan is the foundation on which your entire career change is built. It defines the goals, objectives, procedures, and methods that determine your campaign. It also is a monitoring device that integrates all elements of your marketing mix—telephone, direct mail, networking, and consultants.

We will approach your marketing plan in two phases in this chapter. The first phase is a broad overview of the six parts of a marketing plan, with an example of a successful plan. The second phase is a more detailed discussion geared toward your marketing plan.

Overview of Marketing Plan

Have a blank sheet of paper ready and we will walk through an overview of the information you need to create your marketing plan. First, you need an **objective** for your marketing plan. Your objective describes your ultimate goal. What is the goal of your career change? Are you changing careers to achieve greater advancement? Are you changing careers in order to change your life-style? What kind of industry interests you? Where do you want to work? Write down your objective.

The second part of your plan is **packaging.** Here you want to take a hard look at your physical presentation. Write "Packaging" under your objective.

The third part of your marketing plan is to **define your market.** Write "Market." Under this heading write down the geographical location where you wish to work. Part of defining your market, one of the most critical parts for your campaign, is developing a prospect list. This list is a major tool for you to use in your search, and it consists of company names, addresses, and the name and title of your key contact person in each company. Write "Prospect List" as a subheading under "Market."

The **direct mail campaign** is the fourth part of your plan. It involves writing your resume and a cover letter to send to companies on your prospect list.

The fifth part of your marketing plan is your **network.** Your network consists of family, friends, coworkers, daily business contacts, church and club associates, and many more people you will learn about. Experts say that 75 to 85 percent of all positions are filled through this process.

The sixth and last part of your marketing plan is **personal calls.** These are visits by you to employers either to gather information from a network referral or to seek out a key contact in a company.

You should now have a sheet of paper in front of you that looks something like this:

1. Objective: I want to become a (your career choice).
2. Packaging: Desired image and effort required.

3. Market: Preferred geographic location and type of company.
   a. Prospect List: Names of companies and key contacts.
4. Direct Mail Campaign: List target companies.
   a. Resume: Tailored to specific job and company.
   b. Cover Letter: Directed to specific individual.
   c. Mailings: Sent to target companies.
5. Network: Develop primary, secondary, and tertiary groups.
6. Personal Calls: Prospecting and data gathering.

Now decide the time frame in which you want to accomplish each step. After each listing you must write a date. For example, if you want to accomplish your mid-career change in six months, write the date for six months from now next to your choice of career. Each of the other steps must be completed within that time frame to allow you to achieve your objective. The prospect list must be completed in order to conduct the direct mail campaign. Your resume and cover letter must be written in order to have a direct mail campaign. Your network must be continually worked and expanded in order to generate new contacts.

A well-planned mid-career change marketing campaign helps you achieve your objective because it:

- stimulates your thinking and makes better use of your time and resources;
- highlights your job search responsibilities and schedules your work;
- coordinates and unifies your efforts; and
- creates awareness of obstacles that must be overcome.

To achieve these benefits, your marketing plan should be:

- SIMPLE—easy to understand and conduct;
- CLEAR—precise and detailed;
- PRACTICAL—realistic about objectives; and
- COMPLETE—inclusive of all critical elements.

Sample Marketing Plan

John worked for ten years as the office manager for a large nonprofit organization. He wanted a change to something with more challenge and potential. John was the primary support for his family, so his mid-career change had to be accomplished while he remained employed. What follows is his marketing plan:

1. Objective: Secure a position with a profit-making corporation in the service sector that will allow for personal and professional growth.
2. Packaging: Lose ten pounds and work out at least three times a week.
   a. Sign up for an aerobics class at City College.
3. Market: A distribution company in the same city or local area. Have first job interview within three months. Have one interview per week thereafter with a new prospect, and one or two follow-up interviews. Be employed in a new position within six months from date of plan.
   a. Prospect List: Fifty targeted companies and name of key contact within two months from date of plan.
      (1) Establish a working relationship with three career consultants and/or placement agencies and/or headhunters who specialize in administrative placement. Accomplish within one month.
      (2) Read the local daily paper for information concerning expansion of companies or newly relocated companies. Read the classified ads. Read the weekly business paper for the same information. Make three newspaper-generated telephone calls or personal calls per week.
4. Direct Mail Campaign: Write resume and cover letter within first week of marketing plan. Mail ten sets per week within two weeks.
5. Network: Contact members of my three professional

organizations, local CPAs, attorneys, bankers, and all
salespeople encountered. Develop list of twenty primary contacts within two weeks. Make ten telephone
or personal calls per week to expand the list.

6. Personal Calls: Make at least five calls in person each
week on contacts referred from network.

John had never looked for a position using a marketing plan
or a network. At first, he was not sure how useful a network
would be because he was staying in the same area. John had
targeted being in a new position within six months. He was
able to achieve that goal. To his amazement, it was only
because of his networking that he became aware of the position. It was only through contacts from his network that he
was able to secure a job interview with a consumer electronics
distributor in his city.

Packaging for Success

Not only have you worked for fifteen or more years since you
first looked for a job, but you are fifteen or more years older.
What has that done to your packaging? In the day-to-day
hustle and bustle of work and your other responsibilities, it
has probably been some time since you stood in front of a
mirror and took a critical look at yourself. Now is the time to
get fit. It is not only the fact that you may be competing with
younger people for a job, but when you look and feel your
best, you make a better impression on prospective employers.
Being in the best physical shape also helps you cope with the
stress of working while looking for another position. If you
are not working, good physical shape helps you sustain the
hours that are needed to find your new position. So if you are
like millions of others and have been promising yourself to
start a diet and exercise program, this is the time to start.

There is another part of the physical package that you need
to consider changing at this point—smoking. It is not only
hazardous to your health, but according to *The Wall Street*

Journal, "smoking may be hazardous to your job prospects. A survey by Robert Half International finds that one in four employers would reject a smoker competing for a post with an equally qualified nonsmoker."

You are either middle-aged or very nearly there. Like most of us, you probably have become comfortable with your present looks. There is absolutely nothing wrong with the few gray hairs and wrinkles we have earned going through life. Look at all the living it took to get them! But you may want to reevaluate your overall appearance. Such things as your hairstyle, makeup (women), facial hair (men), and clothes. Are you wearing your hair in the most flattering way possible? A flattering style is more important than the latest style. The same is true of makeup for women. You should wear makeup that is flattering, not overpowering. The test for this is to look at your face in the mirror. If you notice your makeup at first glance, you probably are wearing too much. The acceptance of facial hair on men has changed over the years. Most companies today will tolerate a modest mustache or a well-trimmed beard.

If you are unsure of your reflection in the mirror, ask for an opinion from your spouse or a friend. Make sure that you ask someone who will give you an honest answer. The best place to go for help with your hairstyle (both men and women) is to a professional stylist.

Depending on the job you have now, you may not have the right clothes for your new career. If your new career requires different clothes, invest in one ensemble that is appropriate for your career change. Say, for example, you are now working as a draftsman. You have the engineering background and enough experience to become a representative for a major construction firm. That job requires wearing a well-tailored suit. Your present position requires jeans and a warm sweater for sitting at a drafting board all day. One set of clothes will not set you back too much, and knowing you look the part will give you self-confidence for in-person calls and interviews.

There have been many books and articles written on "dressing for success." They all agree on several basic points:

Men   • Three suits form the core of your wardrobe: a gray chalk stripe, a navy solid, and a gray solid. Shirts and ties create variations.

• Make sure the suits fit you and the shirts look crisp.

Women • Suits and dresses for women should be loose and versatile. A navy blazer that can be worn over a skirt or dress is a good example. Jewelry should be understated and complement your clothing.

Both   • Buy the best you can afford. Choose fewer pieces of higher quality.

• Wear your clothes; your clothes should not wear you.

Defining Your Target Market

You have worked long enough to know the type of environment you want to work in and the type of company you want to work for. You have lived in a geographical area long enough to know whether you want to move or stay. Answer the questions below to define your target market:

• Do you want to stay or move? If you want to move, where to?
• Do you want to work for a large or small company?
• Do you want to work in the public or private sector?
• What kind of product or service do you want to be associated with?
• What kind of management style do you like best to work with?

The answers to these questions target the kind of company you want to work for; add names, and this becomes your prospect list. Flesh out your list with as many company names and key contacts as you can gather. Add to this list over time.

If you are going to stay in the same city or general geographical area, the telephone book, the chamber of commerce, and professional and industry associations can give you listings of firms in the area. If you are relocating, the telephone company can sell you telephone books for other locations.

Sources of information about prospective companies can be found in magazines, newspapers, business journals, and trade publications. The chamber of commerce and other business groups in your targeted area have knowledge about new and growing companies.

A newspaper from the largest city in your targeted geographical area is valuable in several ways. It has employment ads, which give you an idea of current employment trends. It has articles about business growth and changes, employment forecasts, and interviews with managers of companies that either have relocated to the area or are planning to do so in the near future. These articles furnish you with company and contact names. The name may not be that of your key contact, but this person may be able to refer you to the right person.

Business magazines are of help to you for the very same reason, particularly if you are planning to relocate. *Time, Savvy, Newsweek, The Wall Street Journal,* and *The New York Times* are some of the periodicals that have excellent articles about business news and trends across the country.

Appendix A is a list of source books available from the library or your local bookstore. These books list names of companies and associations throughout the country, arranged by industry.

Telephone

Now you have your prospect list, but it probably is not complete. You have the names of companies that you have targeted for your marketing campaign, but you don't have the name of the key contact person. The best contact person is the individual with the power to hire you. If you cannot find the name of that person, you should at least be able to get the name of the supervisor or manager of the department you have targeted. Some sources may list only the owner or president of the business. You can be sure that a telephone call to the president will be directed to the right department. A resume sent to the owner will also end up on the right desk. The names of these individuals may be obtained through sources listed in Appendix A also.

We know people who have worked for a company for twenty years and used the phone only to make lunch reservations. These people do not like to talk over the phone. (They don't understand teenagers at all!) You may be one of these who have never used the telephone to gather information. It may sound hard to do. It's not. Just call the target company. Tell the receptionist that you need the name of the person in charge of your area of interest and the name of that person's supervisor. Before giving the names to you, the receptionist may ask why you need to know. Say that you have information you want to send to them. You don't need to speak to them, you only need their names. If you are transferred directly to one of these people, hang up and call back. You aren't ready to talk to them yet.

A telephone conversation with a receptionist could go something like this:

"Good morning, XYZ Incorporated, may I help you?"

"Good morning. This is [your name]. I have some information I want to send to the manager and supervisor of your doodad department. However, I have only your address. Could you please give me their names?"

"Certainly. Joe Goode is the manager, and Jim Krane is the supervisor of that section."

"Thank you. I will get the information to them right away."

However, as mentioned previously, if you call and are immediately transferred to the department, hang up. When you call back, tell the receptionist you were cut off and need the name of the department supervisor.

The manager and supervisor of a department will be one and

the same in many instances. However, in larger organizations there could be two people or more. The manager may be aware of imminent changes in the company before the supervisor is. The supervisor is usually the person with the final say on hiring. So it's best to contact both.

If you want to relocate and do not want to spend a fortune on long-distance telephone calls gathering information, many of the books in Appendix A can give you contact names.

Once you have a complete prospect list of 50 to 100 companies, you are ready for the next step.

Waging a Direct Mail Campaign

This is one of the best tools for a mid-career changer who is really busy with a current job and a family. A direct mail campaign is an effective tool in your search—but only if you commit yourself to doing it right. There are experts who do not think much of direct mail as a search technique because it succeeds only if it's done correctly. To do it correctly requires more time and effort than many people want to put into it; consequently, many direct mail campaigns fail. The key to its success is your prospect list. Chapter 11 will show you how to write an excellent resume and cover letter, the mailing pieces for your direct mail campaign.

Using your prospect list, select companies to send your resume and cover letter to. Don't mail your resume and cover letter to every company on your prospect list. Select only the companies that are:

• too far away for you to make a personal call;
• large and have personnel departments; or
• ones for which you have been unable to reach the key contact.

Address the cover letter to your key contact person in the target company. The letter and envelope should be typed, not handwritten. Type the word "Confidential" in the lower left-hand corner of the envelope. This usually gets your resume to the right person, bypassing the secretary whose job it is to screen mail for the boss.

Most organizations experience employee turnover at a rate of 20 to 25 percent per year. Large firms have an additional 5 to 10 percent turnover from employees changing jobs internally through transfers or promotions. Your resume may reach an employer just as a vacancy occurs but before it has been advertised. The timely arrival of your resume could result in an interview if you have the qualifications that the position requires.

Only about 15 percent of all companies are large enough to have personnel departments. Direct mail campaigns work well with these companies if your resume bypasses the personnel department, which functions as a gatekeeper. It keeps applicants away from hardworking executives. It also screens all resumes and applications before they are routed to executives with job openings. You may have qualifications that a department needs, but the personnel department usually isn't aware of a planned change in a department until it has an actual job opening. If you send your resume directly to the key contact, it arrives at that crucial time before the position opens to the public.

There is one other reason that direct mail campaigns can have successful results. Many employers would make a personnel change if they knew the right replacement was waiting for the job. Employers are reluctant to fire problem employees who are vital to the operation of the organization, especially when they may have trouble finding a replacement. A vacancy in such a position can adversely affect the whole organization. Your resume could arrive at a company with just such a problem. If you have the right qualifications, you will get an interview.

Networking and Entering the Hidden Job Market

Here is a part of your mid-career change campaign that makes all your years of experience really count over those young sprouts looking for a job. The best networks include people with whom it takes years to become acquainted. A good network of any size needs time to develop.

Only 20 to 30 percent of current job openings are publicly

advertised. Why is this so? How do employers expect to fill vacancies if they do not advertise them?

Put yourself in the shoes of a department head with an opening. Say you are the head of advertising for the local newspaper. You are looking for a new salesperson. You have three positions in the sales department, one of which is now vacant. Your company is a newspaper, so of course, the first thing you do is place an ad in your paper, right? Wrong! The first thing you do is ask the two remaining salespeople if any of their friends are looking for a job. You do this because a great concern of any employer is to hire qualified people who get along well together. If you hire a friend of a current employee, you have a head start. They should get along on the job, and the current employee has a good idea about the friend's qualifications. In other words, by hiring a known quantity, you have cut the risk of hiring someone who will have to be fired because of incompatibility or poor performance. This is the "hidden job market." The key that unlocks the door to the hidden job market is networking.

Networking is the process of reaching out to relatives, friends, and acquaintances and asking them to support your search. Your "network" supports you by providing leads and referrals, and by arranging introductions to others who can provide such information. As your network grows, you come into contact with more people who give you more leads resulting in more interviews and job offers.

You start this process by telling a selected group of your relatives, friends, and acquaintances that you have decided to make a career change. You ask them if they know of any openings in your chosen field, or if they know of anyone who might have such information. This is your primary support group. The people you come into contact with as a result of this primary group become your secondary support group. The contacts you make through the secondary group become your third, or tertiary, group. In this manner your network keeps expanding. Imagine the ripples caused by tossing a pebble into a pond. You are the pebble. Your network is the ever-widening circle of ripples caused by you seeking out contacts.

You may have reservations about this process if you are shy, if you believe people don't like to help, or if you fear a breach of confidence. Fortunately for the human race, particularly for those involved in a job search, people like to help and are usually good about confidentiality. Approached in the right manner, most people are happy to give you information and help you on your way. Why? Because it makes them feel good and they know they may need *your* help someday.

For example, you are about to telephone a secondary contact for the first time. He is a friend of a friend, a person you do not know, but who your friend thinks may have information to help you in your job search. You hesitate to call because he is at work, the head of a department, a very busy man. What you may not know is that this very busy man is a really good friend of your friend. He is busy at a job that keeps him at a desk seven hours a day. Your call may not be an unwelcome interruption; it may make him feel good to be able to help someone who is a good friend of his good friend. In other words, you just might make his day.

Networking Hints

The most effective network is created the moment you leave home and enter college or the work force. That is the reason mid-career changers can have great networks. College friends, particularly those in the same specialty, may supply leads to each other throughout their working lives. The most powerful networks are the result of years of giving and receiving useful information.

Networking should be a process of give and take. That's a key to developing a successful network. Many people take only when they decide to begin networking. Their focus, when they talk to others or meet new people, is: "What can you do for me?" They fail to ask themselves, "What can I do for this person?" How can you give to those in your network? By providing leads and other information that will help them in their businesses. Some of the best leads in your network will come from CPAs, lawyers, bankers, consultants, and salespeople. All of these people are continually building their businesses and careers. They appreciate new business leads. Before you ask someone for a career lead, think about anyone you know who might be able to use their service. Could you introduce or refer them to a prospect? Giving, rather than taking, will get you more time and attention from the busy people in your network.

Show appreciation to the people who help you on your way. Send thank-you notes to those who take time from their busy schedules to talk to you. Keep in touch with your network at regular intervals. You may make a contact who is unable to help you at that moment but who can give you valuable help months later. You don't want to be forgotten.

Personal Calls in Your Marketing Campaign

It is for this part of your mid-career change campaign that we had you reevaluate your middle-aged packaging. Your in-person calls, and later your interviews, can make or break your mid-career change.

In-person calls are not the same as interviews. An interview for a position is the *objective* of your marketing campaign. Personal calls *gather information* for your marketing campaign. When you are making personal calls, make sure it is understood that you are seeking only information, not an interview.

There are two types of personal calls. The first occurs during the phase of your marketing campaign when you are gathering information for your prospect list. The second type of call occurs after you have your prospect list and resume completed, when you want to introduce yourself to prospective employers. You would not want an interview during the first phase, because you don't have enough information yet to be well prepared.

Tips for Successful Prospecting

Never call upon employers before 9:30 in the morning. If you call earlier, they probably are still trying to get their day organized and won't want to be interrupted. End your calls at 11:30 so that you don't interfere with the lunch routine. After-noon calls are best made between 1:30 and 4:00. Don't appear right after lunch; there may be business that came up requiring immediate attention. Calls made after 4:00 will interfere with closing the workday. The best days of the week to make personal calls are Tuesday through Thursday. Monday afternoon and Friday morning are all right—if you have a full week of calls to make. Mondays and Fridays can be very hectic days for many employers. Friday can be busy getting ready for the weekend. Monday is busy with all the things that did not get finished on Friday. This is especially true of companies (such as retailers) that are open for business on the weekend.

A good technique to use for organizing your prospecting calls is the geographic system used by territorial salespeople the world over. The system is called block calling. Get a map of the city you are prospecting and divide it up into blocks or areas. A block should be an area that you can cover in one period of time, such as an afternoon. Number each block and then take out your calendar. Write down a block number for each day you will devote to your search. Now when you look at your calendar, you will know where you intend to be each day for that month. Then you can set up appointments within a block for the same day. You won't have to run to one side of the city for an appointment, and then back to the other side for another. Block calling is systematic, resulting in better coverage. Of course, an important interview may have to be scheduled at the employer's convenience, not yours. You can just change the block calling sequence on your calendar.

As you gather information, you may learn there are no openings within a company. Don't stop there. Make sure to ask if the contact is aware of any possible openings with any other companies. If you make a good impression upon a prospective employer, he may become part of your network. He can give you information about positions in other companies, or forward your resume to another prospective employer.

From time to time you will come upon an employer with a few minutes to spare. If you've made a good impression, he will want to talk to you. Employers call this a preinterview, and it is best avoided if possible. By not being prepared, you may answer the questions poorly and blow the possibility of a more detailed interview at a later time. If a preinterview cannot be avoided, just do your best. One way to avoid this is to tell the prospective employer you have an appointment; then you can set up an interview for a later date.

In Summary

We have covered the six parts of your marketing plan, which is the driving force behind your mid-career change. They are your **objective**, your **packaging**, your desired **geographical location**, your **direct mail campaign**, your **network**, and your **personal calls**. Your direct mail campaign requires a resume and cover letter. The next chapter tells you what you need to know to write them successfully.

Chapter 11

Your Resume as Your Sales Brochure

IN CHAPTER 10 we told you to think of yourself as a product and organize your mid-career change as a marketing campaign to sell that product. Every marketing campaign needs a sales brochure, and yours is no different. Your sales brochure is your resume. Its job is to sell you, to go where you cannot go and say what you don't have the opportunity to say. You want your resume to cause *action!* The purpose of your resume is to get interviews, the action you need to make your mid-career change.

A mid-career changer has three challenges in making a change:

1. To find that new job or career
2. To show skill transferability between different careers and industries
3. To deal with being perceived as overqualified

In this chapter we will discuss how to look for your new career with a selling resume and cover letter. Through a detailed example, we will illustrate how to show skill transferability. Anyone with work experience who makes a job change can run into the "overqualified" objection. We will show you how to minimize the objection and maximize your strengths.

Writing a Resume That Opens New Doors

The key that opens doors is the selling resume. You must understand that there is only one thing people buy, and that is the *benefit* that they can derive from owning or using something. Once you understand this, you will be on your way to successfully selling yourself. To make your mid-career change, *the employer must be able to clearly see the benefit of hiring you.*

How to Write a Selling Resume

If you pick up the typical book about resumes, you see a number of different styles, such as the functional resume, the chronological resume, the analytical resume, and the creative resume. This book recommends one kind of resume: the selling resume.

The selling resume has three main parts:

1. Your career or job objective
2. Your special skills and how the hiring manager can benefit from those skills
3. Your work experience and how it relates to your special skills and qualities

In addition, your name, address, and telephone numbers should be at the top. A list describing your education should be at the end.

Writing your resume will be easier and the results better if you relax and take your time. Be sure to have a thesaurus and a good dictionary by your side. You also need the skill evaluations you produced for Chapter 4. Gather together any information regarding your past employment history, and previous resumes you have written. Now you are ready to begin.

1. Your Career or Job Objective

Your resume should have a career or job objective. Hiring managers are looking for people who want to work for their organization. They want to believe you have a goal in mind that is a good match for the job requirements. If it is not a match, their concern, legitimately, is that you will not be happy in the job and will leave the company prematurely. Replacing you is expensive. A hiring manager would rather not make that kind of mistake. Consequently, they look for resumes that have career or job objectives that are consistent with the job at hand.

Career changers often ask how important it is to customize a resume for a particular job. It is *very important* if you want to be a top contender. Generally, the only part of the resume you must worry about customizing is the objective. (It can be helpful also to customize the skills section.)

When you send letters to placement agencies or recruiters, be sure to have an objective statement general enough to cover the range of jobs that interest you. In your cover letter say that you will be happy to update a resume for a specific job when you become a candidate for that position.

The following are examples of objectives you might use when you tailor your resume for a specific job.

Director of Marketing: Want to join the team of a fast-paced, progressive organization by having a responsible leadership role in the marketing department.

Data Processing Manager: Looking for a challenging department that needs to build communication, foster exceptional customer relations, and create a dynamic team.

Office Manager: Seeking an opportunity to manage an office that will challenge my organizational skills, stimulate my creativity, and test my communication proficiency.

Personnel Manager: Want to join a progressive organization that is concerned with its employees' welfare and looking for an exceptional human resources professional.

Sales Professional: Seeking to join a growing, fast-paced company that rewards its sales professionals for hard work, professional skill, and dedication to the job.

These next job objectives are more general, and could be used when sending your resume to a recruiter.

Senior Manager: Seeking a senior management position that will capitalize on my financial, manufacturing, and marketing skills and experience.

Middle Manager: Looking for a management position that will draw on my past management experience, yet challenge my desire to learn new facets of business in general.

Supervisor: Wish to join a progressive organization as a team leader. Looking for an opportunity to use my accounting skills while gaining broader exposure to the complexities of business.

2. Your Special Skills and How the Hiring Manager Can Benefit from Those Skills

This section is the heart of the Selling Resume. This is where you, as a mid-career changer, have the opportunity to polish those hard-won skills until they shine and stand out.

There are three important stylistic factors to master before you begin writing your resume. First, use **action words.** Second, use **positive** descriptive words. Third, illustrate **benefits.** Employers are looking for motivated, optimistic people who will be a benefit to the company.

Your English teacher asked, "What are action words?" And you of course replied, "Verbs." You must describe your skills with verbs. Following is a list of possible words that you might use.

adapt
administer
analyze
assemble
balance
build
calculate
classify
compare
conceive
coordinate
create
debate
decide
define
detect
direct
document
estimate
evaluate
explain
facilitate
fashion
figure
find
fix
form

govern
identify
imagine
implement
improve
increase
influence
initiate
inspect
interpret
invent
investigate
judge
lead
maintain
manage
moderate
motivate
observe
operate
organize
perceive
perform
persuade
prepare
present
preside

process
program
provide
reconcile
record
recruit
research
review
revise
schedule
screen
select
sell
service
solve
sort
stimulate
structure
summarize
supervise
teach
test
trade
train
win
work
write

Use positive descriptive words, or adjectives, to indicate the level of competency you have in a particular skill. "Excellent" is an example. For instance you may describe a skill as follows:

- Excellent ability to train others in effective customer service
- Excellent communication skills for building strong relationships with my coworkers
- Excellent listening skills for understanding the needs of my customers

This set of examples illustrates the need for more than one word to describe your level of competence. Having read "excellent" once, you get tired of reading it again. This means you must find other words that actively describe each skill. The following list can help you. You can find additional words by using your thesaurus.

able	model
admirable	persistent
commendable	powerful
dynamic	praiseworthy
first-class	special
flexible	strong
forceful	superior
excellent	uncommon
exceptional	unusual
extraordinary	useful
genuine	valuable
meritorious	vigorous

Notice how much more readable the list of skills is after several of the words have been changed.

- Excellent ability to train others in effective customer service
- **Exceptional** communication skills for **building** strong relationships with my coworkers
- **Superior** listening skills for **understanding** the needs of my customers

Finally, describe the benefits an employer will derive from your skill. *A benefit is the result or advantage that can be gained by an employer because you possess a special skill or quality.*

The word "understanding," highlighted above, is not an adjective, it is a verbal. It is used to describe the benefit gained by having "superior listening skills."

In the second skill description, "building" is used to connect the benefit gained from "exceptional communication skills."

Notice that the first skill description did not have a connecting verbal followed by a benefit statement. This is because the benefit of "effective customer service" is going to be clear to the reader without any further description.

Now that you have a list of skills required for a job, a list of positive adjectives describing your competency in each skill, and an understanding of the power of benefits, it is time for you to make a list of *your* special skills.

Begin by looking at the list of skills and knowledge you tabulated in Chapter 4. If your friends helped you, you will have an objective picture of your special abilities. If you did an evaluation without help from your friends, objectivity is our concern. Test your objectivity by remembering a specific situation where you used each skill evaluated. Look at the situation and validate in your mind that the rating you gave yourself was accurate.

Next, ask yourself, "How do these skills relate to the job objective I am pursuing?" Select the skills that fit the objective. Be sure to look at your personal skill evaluations in addition to your professional evaluation. You may find that your job objective will require additional skills.

If you are unsure what skills are appropriate for your new job objective, take the time to talk to someone who is in that line of work. Ask, "What skills are important to make me a success at this job?" Compare your list of skills to what they say. Then select five skills that are most relevant to the job objective and begin writing a skill description for each one. Be sure to use different adjectives to describe your level of competency, and make sure the benefit or advantage of each skill is clearly described. Finally, separate this section on your resume by a border of some kind to make it stand out. See the example resumes at the end of this chapter.

3. Your Work Experience and How It Relates to Your Special Skills and Qualities

Now list your work experience. Most employers are looking for your experience to be listed in reverse chronological order beginning with your present position. Start by listing each job you have had and the dates of each position. If you have worked for only one company, but held a number of jobs within that company, list those jobs with their corresponding dates.

Once you have created this list, begin to evaluate each job by the skill you learned or mastered during that period of time. An example would be: "Improved my persuasive skills." Write that skill next to the job.

Next ask yourself what quantifiable accomplishments were achieved during each job. An example would be: "Saved the company $100,000 by developing an easier way of packing the product." Write these accomplishments next to each job.

After you have developed this list, evaluate the skills and quantified accomplishments in terms of *relevancy* to the job objective stated on your resume. This concentration on *skills* rather than job accomplishments alone will prove you can transfer your talents from one field to another.

Type up a page or two of your jobs chronologically, with their skills and accomplishments. While you review this list look for a logical skill progression from job to job. If the skills and accomplishments do not show you progressing with each job change, reevaluate the skills and accomplishments to be listed for each job. Perhaps you can reorganize the set of skills next to one job and move some to another job, if appropriate, to indicate a progressive level of accomplishment and responsibility. Employers look for progress. They become concerned if it looks like you moved backward with a job change. What they see depends to a large extent upon how you present it. **Do not lie.** That is not what we are saying. Simply create the best picture you can with the paint available.

If the list of jobs you have now typed takes more than one and a half pages, begin reducing it by making shorter lists of accomplishments next to each job. Prioritize what you retain by its *value* to your *job objective*.

A rule of thumb we have developed from talking to hundreds of hiring managers through the years is this: If at all possible, keep your resume to one page. If it must go to two pages, do not fill both pages with margin-to-margin type.

Overqualified?

As a career changer, you may face a problem. Hiring managers could consider you overqualified. They may explain that they would like to hire you but are afraid you will not be happy with a lower-paid position. This can be a problem if you are changing careers and have to begin at the bottom of the ladder. If you have been a senior manager in one line of work, and find that you must begin at the nonmanagement level to learn a new industry, you will meet this problem.

One way to deal with it early on is to reduce or change the type of accomplishments you highlight on your resume. You want your resume to reflect what the reader is looking for. If the reader is looking for nonmanagement people, you cannot change the job titles you held in the past; but you can emphasize the *work* you did rather than the *managing*.

Another way to handle the problem is head on. State in your cover letter that the job would be a career change for you. You expect different responsibilities and less salary, but feel it is worth the price to have the opportunity to pursue a new career field.

How to Show Skill Transferability

We have illustrated the best way to present your skills and experience, but how should you show skill transferability from a career in one industry to a new career in a different industry?

The best way to explain this is with an example of a recent client of ours. Steve Kelly was the manufacturing manager for a company where he had worked for fifteen years. He had worked his way up from the production line into management. But his real dream was to work in television. His family room was full of video equipment. He spent his weekends roaming the city with his camcorder, filming potential news stories. He sold some of his work to local TV news divisions. Steve spent many of his evenings at local cable television studios, doing volunteer producing during public access time. It was during such an evening that he learned about a job opening for a video production manager at a cable station.

Steve's challenge may be yours. He had fifteen years' experience in one industry and wanted to keep his senior equity while transferring to another.

The first thing Steve did was fill out a skills evaluation chart for both jobs. The same chart found in Chapter 4. He listed a task for each skill. Then he compared each skill and listed the similarities between the two jobs. With this list, Steve was able to write his resume relating his current experience as a manufacturing manager specifically to that of a video production manager.

Below is a sample of skills from the Career Skills Evaluation charts, and Steve's evaluation of the tasks performed under each skill category. By studying the example, you can see how Steve used the similarities between each required skill area to write his resume found on page 221.

Manufacturing Manager

Brief job description:

Responsible for the smooth production of a product line through a manufacturing plant.

List of skills required:

Administrative: Devise employee work schedules, including managing peak production time, minimizing use of overtime, and optimizing the productivity of the work force.

Delegation: Supervise the delegated responsibility for employee counseling, discipline, and related personnel matters.

Financial: Calculate return on investment for new equipment acquisitions. Evaluate cost/feasibility for production of proposed products. Manage raw materials and finished goods inventory.

Leadership: Create and share a vision of world-class product manufacturing.

Marketing: No responsibility.

Motivation: Stimulate excitement and enthusiasm to encourage ever-increasing productivity.

Production: Understand and manage material flow and capacity planning.

Project Management: Lead and oversee the completion of projects on schedule and within budget.

Time Management: Simultaneously complete multiple tasks interfacing with many people.

Training Others: Manage and plan training programs for new employees under my supervision.

Video Production Manager

Brief job description:

Responsible for cable television company bids for video production, such as making local television commercials. Manage the production of those projects within bid specifications of time and dollars. Must be able to manage equipment (cameras and lighting), people (actors and technicians), and materials (film and props).

List of skills required:

Administrative: Responsible for employee work schedules, including managing peak production time, minimizing use of overtime, optimizing the productivity of the work force.

Delegation: Minimal delegation, have responsibility for employee counseling, discipline, and related personnel matters.

Financial: Calculate return on investment for new equipment acquisitions. Responsible for computing project bids and assuring desired profit margins.

Leadership: Create and share a vision for top-quality video production.

Marketing: No responsibility.

Motivation: Stimulate excitement and enthusiasm to encourage ever-increasing productivity.

Production: Manage the resources for maximum output.

Project Management: Lead and oversee the completion of projects on schedule and within budget.

Time Management: Complete multiple tasks interfacing with many people.

Training Others: Manage and plan training programs for new employees under his supervision.

Steve Kelly's resume and cover letter, at the end of the chapter, show you how he adapted what he learned from this exercise. The letter highlights the skills the employer requires, and the resume illustrates these skills at work on his present job.

Using Cover Letters and Letters of Introduction to Position Your Candidacy

A cover letter *must* accompany any resume you send through the mail. If you are sending the resume to a friend who you believe will be passing it on to someone else, they will pass on both the resume *and* the letter if you have written a good one.

Most career changers are looking for an opportunity to say something more about their abilities and talents than the standard resume permits. People remark, "If I could just get a chance to talk with the person who will be hiring, I know I could prove my qualifications." The cover letter provides that opportunity.

Abide by seven rules when you write a cover letter.

1. Address the letter to a *person*.
2. Demonstrate your knowledge of the organization and why you are interested in it.
3. Highlight three (if possible) special skills, talents, or

attributes that make you a primary candidate for the company.
4. Be friendly, yet remain professional.
5. Be specific about your intent.
6. Indicate the next step in the process.
7. Be brief, focused, and enthusiastic.

Let us look at each rule in a little more detail.

1. *Address the Letter to a* Person.

We interviewed a number of professional recruiters for this book. When we asked them what was important in a cover letter, their first response was that the letter must be addressed to a person whose name is correctly spelled.

The cost of a telephone call, even from Los Angeles to New York, is cheap if it makes the difference between your letter being read or round-filed.

2. *Demonstrate Your Knowledge of the Organization and Why You Are Interested in It.*

If the letter is going to a company, state your awareness of the company's growth, product, or some other aspect that shows you are knowledgeable about it. This also gives you the opening to tell them the reason you are sending the resume. For example: "Ron Howard told me you are in a dramatic growth mode. He said your shipments have doubled in the past twelve months. I am sending you my resume because Ron indicated you are looking for people with energy and enthusiasm who are willing to work in the chaos of a growing company."

3. *Highlight Three (If Possible) Special Skills, Talents, or Attributes That Make You a Primary Candidate for the Company.*

Look at the section on your resume for special skills and qualities. Think of another way to present those skills specifically for this job application.

For example, on your resume you have a skills statement that reads:

"Exceptional financial management skills with a special ability to control costs."

If you apply for a job as chief financial officer, this point in your cover letter could read:

"I am known as an **expert** in cost control with a problem-solving approach. I look for creative solutions to cost control rather than simply say no to expenditures."

A second example is that of applying for the job of office manager. On your resume, you have a skills description that reads:

"Dynamic 'take charge' attitude demonstrating strong leadership skills."

The highlighted point in your cover letter could read:

"I am highly **motivated** and willing to accept responsibility for getting things done. This attitude helps me motivate others to be creative, assertive, and dependable."

It is important to be thinking *benefits*. You must get the reader's attention quickly by highlighting two or three key characteristics that would describe a top candidate for the position. We recommend you draw attention to these points by using either an asterisk in front of each of the key statements or by using boldface type for the key word in each statement. Also be sure to set each statement apart by spacing. Do not put all of the statements into one paragraph. They lose their punch. Besides, a large paragraph will not draw the reader's attention.

You must get the attention of the reader *immediately*. A busy hiring manager who has to read thirty letters for each opening is going to only skim each one. This is the reason for separating the section of special skills/personal strengths with a dramatic border on your resume and using asterisks or boldface type in your cover letter. If you fail to do these things, you greatly reduce the chances of your resume making a lasting impression.

4. Be Friendly, Yet Remain Professional.

If you are sending the letter to someone with whom you have established a good rapport, address the letter "Dear Bob." If you have not talked to the person, address the letter "Dear Mr. Wade."

Avoid using too many cute phrases, but also avoid sounding like a lawyer. Do not say, "Enclosed please find my resume." Say, "I have enclosed my resume."

Be careful about gimmicks. They can backfire. However, being creative can be just the ticket if the job for which you are applying is one that demands a creative touch. Make sure your approach is appropriate. If you have questions about what is appropriate, talk to the receptionist. They will know what works within the office and usually will be very willing to help.

5. Be Specific About Your Intent.

Do not send a vague "testing the waters" letter. It will simply end up in the round file. Let the person know why you are sending the letter. Say that you have heard about an opening and wish to apply. Or that you have heard about the company and want to know what employment possibilities exist for a person with your talents. Sometimes a company will take the time to interview a talented individual even if there are no current job openings. This happens only when a candidate has researched a company, discovered specific areas of interest, and addressed those areas with a carefully written cover letter and a well-targeted resume. Within that resume, each item listed clearly states the benefits to be derived for the company.

6. Indicate the Next Step in the Process.

That next step must be an action *you* take. For example, close the letter with, "I will call you next week to see if you have any questions about my qualifications." A second example is: "I look forward to speaking with you about the job opportunity. I will call you next Wednesday."

Do not leave the letter just hanging in the air. Do not expect the recipient to take the next step. Be sure you clearly indicate an action, such as telephoning, and that you will be the one to take it. If you *do* get a call, count it as a lucky stroke. That is not the way it will usually work.

7. Be Brief, Focused, and Enthusiastic.

Finally, keep it simple. Of course there are pages and pages of wonderful things you could write about yourself. Save such a detailed enumeration for the interview. *Remember,* your resume and cover letter have just *one* job, to sell a hiring manager on an interview. The reader of your resume and cover letter does not care how wonderful you are. The reader cares only about *what you can do for them or their company.* The reader is looking for a person who will fulfill *their needs, not yours.* Remember that the reader never has a lot of time. Keep the letter brief and to the point.

Smile when you write your cover letters. You want your letters to reflect your enthusiasm and motivation.

Sample Winning Resumes & Letters of Introduction

The following pages offer examples of resumes and cover letters of actual people. The names of the individuals and company names and addresses have been changed to assure confidentiality, yet the information is real. These are winning resumes; each was instrumental in making a mid-career change for the writer.

After you have studied the examples, you are ready for the next chapter, which deals with the objective of your resume and cover letter: the all-important interview.

(Same Industry, Same Career)————————————

Sandy E. May
1234 29th
Longview, WA 98632
206-555-1212

SPECIAL SKILLS AND QUALITIES

* A positive attitude and high energy level allow me to readily motivate those I work with.
* My tenacious nature gives a high return in territory development dollars.
* Excellent communication skills help me to easily work with diverse groups of people.

CAREER OBJECTIVE

A challenging position in sales with an expanding organization offering opportunities to utilize my special strengths and industry knowledge.

PROFESSIONAL EXPERIENCE

3/84–5/85

THE DAILY NEWS, Longview, WA. Outside Classified Salesman. Created my own territory and account list of 35 plus. Researched nonadvertisers, created speculative layouts, worked out budgets, then called on them cold. Sold two special sections and various special multiadvertised ads. I was cross-trained at my own request, in the phone room and on a computer.

9/74–3/84

HOLIDAY INNS, INC., Kansas City, MO. Sales Representative. Researched the Kansas City Metropolitan area making cold calls and selling new accounts. Also worked with companies out of the area booking conferences and conventions in our facility.

EDUCATION

4/84 PNANCAM Phone Room Class
2/75 Sales Course, Holiday Inn University

November 27, 1985

Jim Wilson
District Sales Manager
Seattle Times, Inc.
PO Box 306
Seattle, WA 96111

Dear Mr. Wilson:

High-performance sales professionals are always in demand. Experience has shown me that good positions can be found even in tough times for those who have the talent.

Currently, I am working for a small company and I am the number-one sales rep. I have found that my ability to make a maximum contribution to the company is limited due to their size. As a result, I have begun a discreet search.

My strengths are:

1. **exceptional** new accounts developer
2. outstanding **knowledge** of the **sales** process
3. consistent **top performer**

Please consider this letter an application for a direct sales position for your eastern territory. My base salary for 1985 is $16,800; by the end of the year my earnings (salary plus commission) will be at least $48,000. A new position should offer comparable earning opportunities.

I will call you next Tuesday. I look forward to speaking with you shortly.

Thank you for your time.

Sincerely,

Sandy E. May

SEM/jn

(Industry Change, Same Career)_____

Clark R. Walker
4809 SE River Road
Milwaukee, WI 53111

Home: 414-555-1214   Work: 414-555-1213

CAREER OBJECTIVE

A challenging general management position in a growth industry, offering the opportunity to capitalize on my international finance, manufacturing, and marketing skills.

✳✳✳

PERSONAL STRENGTHS

* Dynamic leadership skills, high energy level, and a commitment to achieving aggressive goals.
* Excellent communication skills allowing me to build strong relationships with bankers, vendors, and customers.
* Exceptional strategic planning, delegation/training, and listening skills.

✳✳✳

EXPERIENCE

Present: Vice Pres/CFO, Secretary, Treasurer, Member of Board of Directors, Acting General Manager, CAPITAL IMPORTS CORP. Team leader for the negotiation of an LBO. Lead acquisition/transition of GTT Consumer Products Company. Negotiated $40 million line of credit. Responsible for daily operation of a $100+ million business.

74–85:   Finance Manager, CENTRAL DIVISION/CPI (Container Packaging Inc.) Financial and business planning management responsibilities, reporting to the general manager. Division annual revenue, $350 M.

71–74:   Manager Business Planning, FOOD DIVISION/CPI; Chicago, IL. Responsible for financial evaluation of new products, profitability of existing products, competitive pricing, and new and expanded facilities. Division annual revenue, $500 M.

64–71:   Coordinator, MIS, EASTERN METAL DIVISION/CPI; New York, NY.

62–64:   Supervisor, EDP, PATERSON DATA CENTER/CPI; Paterson, NJ. Became supervisor after completion of management training program.

EDUCATION

* B.S. Business Administration, Fairmont State College
* Postgraduate work, Northern Illinois University
* Executive Management Program, Northwestern University
* Various IBM data processing courses

October 9, 1990

Harold A. Russell
Senior Vice President
Harold Russell & Associates
777 Fifth Avenue
New York, NY 10111

Dear Hal:

Thank you for your letter informing me of your new position. Due to recent changes at Capital Imports Corp., such as my ownership position being bought out and Mike Davis no longer being president, I would appreciate it if you would give consideration to my resume for any appropriate position you have open within your client companies.

For your information, I have three significant capabilities that are not reflected on my resume:

* Extensive work in **international finance** for offshore manufacturing.
* Heavy involvement with **securing** and **continuing** the **investment relationship** between CIC and Mason Capital Interfunding. This connection offers me an open door for a future interfunding relationship if I were to join another company looking for financing to enlarge its business. (I have been told by others that Bill MacGregor, a senior vice president with Mason Capital Interfunding, considers me the best CFO in MCI's portfolio of companies.)
* Nearly seven years of **ownership** of two **retail outlets** that sold White Water overproduction, one in Chicago, IL, and one in Vancouver, WA.

I am looking for an opportunity to become general manager or president of a company. (I've been acting in that capacity for 18 months.) I'm known as a "team builder" and a "problem solver." I have done wonders for cost controls at CIC. My method of controlling costs is to look for alternatives and creative solutions rather than to simply say no to expenditures.

My current compensation is a base salary of $150,000 plus bonus, car allowance, and fitness club.

If you believe there could be a mutually beneficial opportunity for a client, please give me a call at 414-555-1214. Thank you for your time.

Sincerely,

Clark R. Walker

(Career Field Change)_____

Steve Kelly
1234 SW Fernwood Dr.
Los Angeles, CA 91111

Work: 213-555-1215   Home: 213-555-1216

OBJECTIVE:

A challenging video production manager position with a growth-oriented cable television company that needs my current skills and will allow me to grow professionally.

****

SPECIAL SKILLS AND QUALITIES:

* Exceptional knowledge of and skill with the complexities of project management.
* Flexibility, innovation, and multi-task orientation make me adaptable to varied and hectic work environments.
* Excellent leadership skills, high energy level, and commitment to achieving goals. These qualities help me motivate those with whom I work.

****

1980–Current:

MANUFACTURING MANAGER—ABC International Widget Company
Responsibilities include: Management and cost control for a 20-person manufacturing team, processing 300+ orders per day during peak season. Shipments are distributed both nationally and internationally with responsibility for customer service.

Stock inventory control includes managing approximately 150 product styles and 150,000 to 200,000 items in stock at any given time. Continually develop and manage new techniques for product quality control. Work with raw material suppliers and accessory manufacturers to improve quality of items, eliminating lost time due to defects in materials and workmanship.

Warranty department responsibilities include repair or replacement for up to 100 items daily. Often personally handle irate customers.

Packaging department continually develops and designs improved packaging/container products. Strong vendor relationships allow for the continued innovation.

Design and manufacture product displays and custom cabinets used in trade shows and retail outlets. Interaction with customers has allowed me to refine and improve display designs.

Design and review training programs for new employees.

1974–1976:

MAINTENANCE ENGINEER/MARINA SUPERVISOR— Long Beach Corp.
Responsibilities included facilities and power plant operation, water flow and quality, and daily operation of the marina.

EDUCATION

1974–75:   Pasadena Community College.

Numerous supervisory management classes and seminars.

December 27, 1990

Jay Davison
General Manager
Metropolitan Cable Company
PO Box 306
Long Beach, CA 92111

Dear Mr. Davison:

Thank you for your time on the telephone. Your company has a reputation for developing employee potential and consistently expanding sales. Both of these qualities attract me to you. It is my desire to become an expert in video production management. I'm looking for an opportunity to work for an organization that is interested in retaining the best people through effective leadership and commitment to quality.

My strengths are:

1. **Extensive** knowledge of **project management,** including bringing projects in on time and within budget.
2. Solid management and **motivational** skills.
3. Commitment to achieving **top** management **goals.**

One strength that does not show on this resume is the time I have invested in learning the video production business. For the past five years I have worked with cameras, lighting, and stage management. I have also edited 15 thirty-minute cooking programs presented on a local cable channel.

This letter and my resume are an application for your open position for a video production manager.

I will call you next Friday, as we agreed. I look forward to speaking with you soon.

Thank you again for your time.

Sincerely,

Steve Kelly

SEK/jn

Chapter 12

Interviews That Get the Job

As a rule, mid-career changers have had fewer recent interviews than their younger competitors. Even so, mid-career changers have a distinct edge: **They know more about business.** The interview is your opportunity to demonstrate your edge. This chapter shows you how to get the information you need, lets you know what questions to expect, and shows you how to prove your superior credentials in an interview.

It's Okay to Be Afraid

The average person in your shoes hasn't had any kind of interview for at least five years. Most have not had an outside job interview for fifteen years or more. If your palms sweat just thinking about an interview, you're normal. The first thing you should do is let yourself know it's okay to be afraid; then deal with the fear.

Dealing with Fear at Its Root

We are taught fear, we are not born with it. Watch a six-*month*-old child; you will see that he is afraid of nothing. Talk to a six-*year*-old child and you will learn that he can't speak to strangers and he's afraid to go down the street alone.

As a parent, you can understand the need to teach children to be careful. Yet learned fears carry over into adult life. They manifest themselves in such ways as the fear of meeting new people, trying something new, making a mistake, or being less than a success.

Actually, fear is caused by insufficient information. Prejudice is an example. The word means prejudgment—making a judgment before the fact. Prejudice is usually overcome with information and experience. Many members of different races are afraid of one another, but when they have personal experience through schools, the workplace, or the armed services, they learn that they have more similarities than differences. When they get to know each other, they eliminate the fear.

Approach your job search fears, especially that of interviewing, in the same manner. Gather information; information is power. It will enable you to know what to expect, how to respond, and how to look more professional than your competition.

Many have written and talked about the fear of rejection. It has been turned into a bigger monster than it really is. Rarely is a job applicant personally rejected. Most of the time a person is rejected because of inadequate background, a lack of skill, or insufficient training for the job. Because these are the reasons for rejection, the problem is manageable. You can polish your skills and expand your knowledge. You can also minimize the importance of a missing or insufficient skill by focusing the hiring manager's attention on an *important* skill that you do have. (This technique is explored later in the chapter.)

The bottom line is this: information reduces fear. You won't be rejected if you are prepared. You may lose a prospective job to a candidate with better credentials, but that should be rare; your years of experience give you the edge. You'll prove that edge by being the *best* job interviewee.

How to Prepare for Success

Fail to prepare and you prepare to fail. That is more true than ever when interviewing. Adequate preparation quells your fears and shows you're the best candidate. The logical question is then "What do I prepare *for* and how do I *do* it?"

You prepare for the interview by learning as much as you can in three areas: the employer's skill needs and requirements, the company's background and culture, and the interviewer's personal tastes and characteristics.

Employer's Skill Needs and Requirements

We have discussed a lot about skills. As a mid-career changer, you know you have a broader collection of skills to offer. When you prepare for a *specific* interview, it is time to be adept at illustrating your proficiency in the *specific* skills the job requires. The more you can learn about the job requirements, the easier you will handle questions regarding your ability to address those needs.

There are several ways to get this information. First, talk in depth with the human resources person assigned to fill the job. Their knowledge can range from knowing a simple job description to being intimately acquainted with the job and its requirements.

Ask questions of the human resources person with the assumption that they are knowledgeable. If they don't have the information you need, they can help you locate someone who does. Remember, their job is to send on *qualified* candidates. The more you ask about the job requirements, the more confident the human resources person will be that you are a superior candidate.

Below are the most important questions to ask a human resources person. Feel free to add to this list, on the basis of your own experience.

1. In general, what does the job entail?
2. How has this job been filled in the past?

3. What *specifically* made the previous person successful in the job?
4. What *specifically* could have been done to improve job performance?
5. If you were the hiring manager, what *one* characteristic would you consider most important in a candidate for this position?
6. What special *skills* did the previous person have?
7. What personal qualities make people successful around here?

Once you have this information, you are ready to present your skills in terms that *correspond directly* to the qualifications the *employer* indicated were necessary.

Company's Background and Culture

The human resources person can give you extensive information and background on the company. Many companies have packets of information already prepared for new employees and job applicants. If a packet is not offered, ask for one. If the human resources department can't help you, the marketing department probably can. Tell them you are interviewing for a job and that you want to be as well prepared as possible. The information you are looking for is a marketing department's stock-in-trade. Do your best to get everything on the following list:

1. Product brochures
2. News releases for the past year
3. Annual report and 10-K report, if the company is publicly held
4. Any newsclips about the company from the past five years
5. Customer support materials
6. Several issues of the company's newsletter

This information can do two things for you. It can help you get a feel for the company: its corporate culture, its employee relations, its commitment to customer service, and its product quality. It can also help you understand the company's history. Is the company growing? Has it recently changed direction? Is it developing new products and services and staying competitive?

Asking for information shows that you are seriously interested in the job. And the knowledge will help you present yourself as being attuned to the company's style.

Last but not least, learning more about the company helps you determine if this is the company *you* want to join. You're making an important change; don't short-circuit it by failing to confirm that the company fits your needs.

Interviewer's Personal Taste and Characteristics

Before your first interview, do your best to determine who will be interviewing you during the hiring process. Generally, there will be three to five interviews before a job offer is made. (Because you are a more senior person, occasionally there could be more than that.) When you learn who the interviewers are, gather all the personal information you can find about each individual.

A person who can help you in this is the interviewer's administrative assistant. Assistants usually are very willing to help you understand their boss's personal characteristics. Tell the assistant you will be interviewing and ask for help. Use a story, if possible, to illustrate the benefit of being helpful. You're an experienced manager, tell the person how your assistant prepared job candidates you used to interview, and how this helped the interviewing process flow more smoothly: job candidates arrived for the interview more relaxed and better prepared, and this made things easier for everyone involved. Use your experience edge in this situation.

If you're running into a brick wall, try talking to other employees within the company or department. You want to make a good impression on the interviewer; you need answers to the following questions:

1. Approximately how old is the boss?
2. How does the boss dress?

3. What is their background? Where did they go to school?
4. What does the assistant like best about working for them?
5. What challenges does the assistant face working with them?
6. What type of people seem to get along best with the boss?
7. What would be the single most important thing you could do to make a good impression?

You ask these questions because you want to know what to expect, how to dress, and how to prepare.

Sometimes you can't get all the information. But you will be surprised how forthcoming secretaries and assistants are if you ask. Most job seekers don't ask, so they go into interviews unprepared and afraid. Now you see how you can be both prepared and unafraid.

What You Can Expect and How to Deal with It

If you have not looked for a job recently, there are two developments that may surprise you: drug testing, and ethics and personality tests. Here are a few tips to keep you from getting flustered by these new developments.

Dealing with Drug Tests

You didn't take a drug test before your first job, and you may consider drug testing an invasion of privacy. Unfortunately, drugs are such a pervasive problem, employers are forced into testing. One of our clients recently started drug testing because the neighboring companies were doing it and word was on the street that his company didn't test. As a result, a deluge of drug users and pushers had made their way into his factory. When the company announced testing, a number of employees left and never returned. Those who remained were happy to see the improvement. Our advice is to be ready to take a drug test and understand the employer's need to give it.

Handling Ethics and Personality Tests

You may think it is tough to find a good job; it is just as tough to find quality employees.

Employers face an array of legal barriers that prevent them from getting important personal background information from prospective employees. If you were a hiring manager, you would be much more concerned than the prospective employee about the hiring process. A hiring manager may put their job on the line with each new hire. They have a great deal of responsibility. The person they hire can jeopardize the company's profits and can affect the working environment of other employees. Is it any wonder that employers are constantly looking for ways to make the process more successful?

Testing has gained popularity, because testing companies promise their tests will weed out bad job prospects. Today preemployment tests include ethical tests asking questions like this: "Have you ever stolen from an employer? Would you be tempted to use your employee discount for a friend?"

Preemployment personality tests may ask you questions about your decision-making process, your habits, and your values. They may also ask you about the habits in others that bother you, and why you are motivated to do what you do.

When you are presented with a test by a prospective employer, your best approach is to be as positive about the situation as possible (some employers judge your reaction to the test as closely as they evaluate your test results), and to answer the questions as honestly as you can. If you are ruled out for a job based on your test results, remember that it may be better for you in the long run. You probably would not have fit in with the company's style and it is better to find that out up front.

Questions . . . a Key to Your Success

The prework having been done, it's time to deal with the actual interview. Questions are the heart of the interview, both the questions you answer and the ones you ask. That's right, you must be prepared to ask questions, too. The employer should not be asking all of the questions. You can't make an effective presentation demonstrating your skills until you have asked enough questions to know *how* and *what* to present.

Let's step back a moment and look at why employers hold interviews. They are looking for *proof* of who is the best candidate. An interview is an opportunity to *sell your skills*. You sell by matching the needs of the *company* to your superior skills, *proving* that you are the best candidate.

Asking Questions and Controlling the Process

Now that you recognize you are selling, you need to understand the sales process. The buyer goes through a predictable process:

1. Rapport is built between the seller and the buyer. Each becomes comfortable with the other's integrity.
2. The seller looks for the buyer's specific needs.
3. The buyer looks for proof that his needs can be met.
4. The buyer makes a decision to act (makes the job offer).

As the seller, you want the action to be a job offer. Again, as a mid-career changer, your business experience works in your favor. You can relate to what we are saying below. It means more to you, so you can more easily put it to work.

1. Building Rapport

Here is an example of a typical interview.

"Hello, John. Thank you for coming in today."

John, the job applicant, shakes hands with the interviewer and sits down.

"John, why don't you tell me about yourself."

"Oh," John says as he shifts in his chair and looks down at his feet, "my last job . . . ."

What do we see? Two people who are uncomfortable and trying to get to know each other. The interviewer tries to make John comfortable by getting him to talk. John is not really comfortable with that because he does not know what he should talk about. This interview can be totally different if John comes in prepared to help the interviewer with the process.

"Hello, John. Thank you for coming in today."

John, extending his hands, says, "Thank you for giving me your time," glances around, and takes a seat.

"That's an interesting painting behind your desk," John observes. "Where did you get it?"

"Isn't it great? I was stationed in Alaska for two years . . ."

What has happened now? First of all, John has taken charge of building rapport. He has identified something unique within the interviewer's office and asked an open-ended question, getting the interviewer talking and making both of them comfortable.

You have heard how important the first thirty seconds of an interview are. Whom would you hire? The first John, shifting in his chair, not knowing what to say, or the second John, who extended his hand and got you talking?

By using your abilities to appear confident and to break the initial tension, you accomplish the first (and sometimes most important) phase of selling yourself. You begin to build rapport.

2. Identifying Needs

Once you have built rapport, your next step is to understand the specific needs that must be met to get an offer.

Again, look at the typical job interview.

"John, on your last job, did you have responsibility for supervising the accounting department?"

"Yes, I had twelve people reporting to me," John responds, thinking he can now talk about how many people he managed.

"I see," the interviewer says. "Well, this job won't have accounting reporting directly to it." Now the interviewer wonders if John will be the right person for the job.

Now look at the interview when John is guiding it.

John has learned several pieces of information about his prospect by now. He found out that Kurt, the interviewer, spent time in Alaska and goes up there every summer for fly-fishing. John likes fly-fishing, too, so they discuss several fly patterns they both like to tie. The personal chat is slowing down and John knows it is time to move on to the business at hand.

"Kurt, I've had the opportunity to look at some of your product literature, and it looks like you have several leading-edge items. Tell me, what exciting things do you see happening in the near future?"

"I'm glad you asked. The reason you are in here today is because one of those products you looked at has grown so fast that we are having to set up a separate division just to handle the volume."

"How do you plan to set that division up?" John asks, guiding Kurt in the general direction of the job.

John next asks Kurt, "What responsibilities will be assigned to this new position?"

Then John will ask, "What do you feel are the essential characteristics a person in this position should have?"

He will follow that question with, "What makes managers in your company successful?"

Then, "What can hurt a manager's success?"

If information is power, John is now in a powerful position. Without doing much talking himself, John has made Kurt comfortable. John is poised and professional, and he has learned the key characteristics that Kurt is looking for in a new manager.

John now understands the needs of the company. He is ready to present proof to Kurt that he is the best candidate for the job.

Before we move on, take another look at the questions John asked. John first asked a general question that gave him a feel for the company. It was an upbeat question: "What exciting things do you see happening in the near future?" Then John moved Kurt into more specific questions relating directly to the job. From these questions he learned what Kurt needed in a manager and what Kurt felt would be unsuccessful. John has the job if he can *prove* to Kurt that he can meet those needs.

3. Presenting Proof of Your Abilities

Now John has to prove to Kurt that he is the person for the job. He does this in two ways. First, John uses Kurt's words and descriptions of the skills required. John shows Kurt that he has those skills. Second, John *demonstrates* his skills at work by telling a short story. The story is about a time when John applied several of his management skills to bring a difficult situation to a successful conclusion.

Kurt needs a new division manager with an exceptional ability to work with people over whom he has no authority. The division will be small, forcing it to use the services of the central office for accounting, administrative support, and data processing. New systems will have to be designed to support several unique aspects of the division, and the manager will have to adapt and manage the installation of existing accounting methods within the division.

"The job sounds interesting," John says as he thinks about the challenges facing this new position. "Before I took my current job, I had to deal with a similar situation. I was a lead analyst for data processing and I had the assignment of designing a new sales reporting system. The vice president of sales had given me extensive report-generating requirements. The data needed to create these reports was not being gathered by the corporate system. That meant that I had to go to several overworked departments and ask them to begin gathering additional information. The resistance was high. I did my homework and showed each group how this added information would give them a better understanding of some of their own problems. Once they saw some benefit in making the change, they were willing to do the work.

"I've learned how important it is to show people how they can benefit from a change rather than trying to strong-arm them into action. It may take a little longer, but once they see the benefit, they'll invest the effort making your project a success.

"You know, it's really just like fishing. That fish is wild. He doesn't have to take your bait. You have to find what he wants to get him to do what you want. When you find his bait, you've got him.''

Look at John's approach. The number-one characteristic Kurt was looking for was a proven ability to work with others. John's story didn't even relate to his most recent job. It didn't have to. He simply needed to *prove* that he had the skill Kurt was looking for. Then John related that ability to something personal he and Kurt had already discussed. Tying the skill back to fishing increased the value to Kurt. That personal hook guaranteed that Kurt could relate to what John was saying.

If John's competitors demonstrate the same qualities regarding people management, but do not relate those qualities to something personal such as the fly-fishing, then their demonstration will not be as strong. In the end when Kurt evaluates the strengths of each candidate, he is much more likely to *remember* what John said.

There are two things to remember for proving your value to the hiring manager. First, it is people who hire you, not companies. Relate the value or benefit of a specific skill in terms that will be meaningful to the individual interviewing you. Second, remember that the interviewing person really is not looking for the skill as much as the benefit that results from your possession of the skill. That means your story can't stop with a demonstration of the skill, it must continue until you have clearly illustrated the *results*. In John's story, he demonstrated the benefit by saying he found that people would do the agreed work and "invest the effort making your project a success" if they saw a positive reason for doing what they needed to do.

Kurt could relate directly to this benefit, because the management skill he needed to see proven was the ability to get things done without specific authority while not making people angry.

Look at your skills. Then search for a story that demonstrates each skill at work. As a mid-career changer, you have years of stories to draw upon. Like John, you need not worry if the best story you find isn't one from your most recent job. The point is to find a story that is easy to remember and easy to understand. Practice telling these stories to friends, and adapt your conclusion to something personal that your friend can identify with. Practice, practice, practice. Storytelling is a skill in itself and one of the most important skills you can develop if you want to become the best interviewee.

4. Getting the Offer

Before John can close this interview, he must learn just who has the hiring authority. In other words, you should never ask someone to make a job offer if they do not have the authority, or if they have a commitment to interview additional candidates. They won't want to give you an answer, and if you push, you may blow a potential offer.

This means that you must *qualify* the situation before you take the next step. There is one question John must ask now: "Kurt, what is the decision process for filling this job?"

Before you close the interview, you must know three things.

1. You must know *who* will make the final decision.
2. You must know *when* the decision is going to be made.
3. You must know *how* the candidates will be evaluated.

The question "What is your decision process?" covers all three areas. Once you uncover the decision process, you can close the interview appropriately.

For example, Kurt has told John that he has the final say in the selection of the new employee. But two other managers are going to interview each candidate, just to be sure the chemistry is right. John's first interview has been with Kurt, so he now knows how he must close in order to get the *next interview*. He can handle it like this:

> "Kurt, I'm excited about your company, and the job sounds like an interesting challenge. When can I meet the other managers?"

John uses a simple, assertive, and positive closing technique. He knows that Kurt feels good about him, and he knows that Kurt is not ready to offer him a job. The logical step is to ask for the next interview. If John asks for the job without qualifying the situation, he could lose the rapport with Kurt. If John doesn't ask for the next step, Kurt might think John is too timid to do the job. By knowing what to do, John is able to move smoothly to his desired conclusion.

Time passes and now John is further along in the process. He has already interviewed with the other managers; he feels he did well with both of them. He has another interview with Kurt, who tells John that he expects to make a decision soon. Kurt indicates that he has one other candidate to interview. John handles the situation this way:

> "Kurt, I'm excited about this opportunity. I felt good with Alan and Joe, and they must have felt good about me or I wouldn't be here. I know you have another interview this afternoon. You said you want to make a decision by Friday. That means you will be considering the candidates tomorrow. May I call you tomorrow afternoon to answer any questions that may arise during your evaluation process?"

> "I'm going to be in a meeting all afternoon, so I won't be available."

"Then why don't I call you first thing Friday morning," John says, not wanting to leave the last move up to Kurt.

"Okay, that will be fine. I'll talk to you then."

"What's the best time to get you?" John asks, closing the loop.

"I'm in by eight, and that's when the switchboard opens."

"Great, I'll talk to you then."

In this scenario, John demonstrated interest and assertiveness. He respected Kurt's timing and need to have one more interview. The one subtle control John retained is the follow-up call. Kurt may have questions *prior* to making his decision. This means that even though Kurt wants to make the decision by Friday, John still has a chance to answer questions and deal with any objections resulting from the interview with the other candidate.

Chances are the other person will not be in control of the situation. Most job applicants are timid and allow the interviewer to control the process. By his retaining control, John increases his chance of closing the sale in his favor.

Responding to Interview Questions

The contrast between the two Johns' interviews illustrates how you can use questions to control the interviewing process. To give you even more of an advantage, let's look at five questions often in the mind of interviewers.

1. What kind of person are you?
2. Do you have good management/people skills?
3. What are your business or technical skills?
4. What is your attitude toward work and life?
5. How motivated are you?

The interviewer is trying to get an accurate picture of who you are. By using good questioning skills (as "the second John" did) you can give the interviewer answers to many of his questions without his having to ask specifics. John's assertive control showed Kurt that he was a positive, highly motivated person. The questions John asked showed good business sense. The story illustrated John's skills as a manager.

Clearly, John's ability to manage the interview process was at an expert level. You may not be at that level, so you need to be prepared to answer questions similar to the following.

1. What Kind of Person Are You?

Employers know they hire the whole person. They hire your likes, dislikes, habits, quirks, attitudes, and prejudices. They ask questions designed to uncover what is important to you. They need to know if your values will fit in with the company. Here are examples of what you can expect.

a. How can you make a contribution to our company? You cannot answer this question well unless you know something about the company. If you did your homework and learned about the company before the interview, or if you started the interview out with the question "What exciting things are happening . . ." you would have information about the company that would prepare you for an answer. Otherwise, before responding to this query, you must ask a qualifying question to gather information, such as: "I take pride in the contribution I've made everywhere I've worked. I'd have to understand the job responsibilities more clearly before I could give you a specific answer to that. What responsibilities and objectives have been set for the job?"

b. What has been your biggest accomplishment? The interviewer asking this question wants to get a feeling for your self-image. They are looking for objectivity and confidence. Do not overdramatize what you have accomplished. Babe Ruth said, "If I did it, it ain't braggin'." Yet it is important that you really did do it. If you were the member of a successful team of people, recognize the team's accomplishments and give yourself credit for having learned a lot in that association.

c. What is your greatest strength? This you can answer with ease. You have assessed your strengths, and that assessment has been through the eyes of others. Tell the interviewer about your assessment process and give a story that illustrates successful results when those strengths are applied in a work situation.

d. Why are you interested in working for our company? This is a great question if you have done your homework. You can compliment the company in the process of responding. But also answer this question by focusing on challenges and opportunities you see facing the company, and show that you want to tackle those issues. Many people want to leave a company with problems and find one with fewer difficulties; in other words, they don't want to work as hard as they have been. This can come across as a "clock watcher" attitude in an interview, and this question is geared to uncover that attitude.

e. Why should we hire you? If you have gathered enough information during the interview process, you can answer this question simply and directly. It gives you an opportunity to summarize the company's needs and then state your qualifications, possibly concluding with another short illustrative story.

f. Why are you out of work? Be honest and be positive. If you were laid off, explain why. If you were fired, admit it and tell what you have learned from the experience. Many successful CEOs, such as Lee Iacocca, were once fired from a job. Just be sure you learned something that will be helpful in the future. Then move on. Focus on your desire to make a contribution.

2. Do You Have Good Management/People Skills?

John illustrated his people skills through his data processing story. He then reinforced it by relating it to fishing. The single most important quality needed in managers today is effective people skills. The following questions are examples of what you might be asked.

a. What kind of people give you problems as a manager and why? Unfortunately, almost every department is stuck with someone who is unmotivated or who causes problems. Often these people have been in their job for a long time and they have special skills that are hard or costly to replace. This question is designed to understand how you will deal with someone like this. If you are a progressive manager, you will look for a new way to motivate this person. Just like John, you know that all people have something that can make them enthusiastic. As the manager of such an employee, you will look for that special motivation that can spark their interest in their job. Relate a story about someone you managed in this manner.

b. Describe your relationship with your boss. This is an opportunity to give a positive and direct comment. *Do not, under any circumstance, say something negative about your boss or your company.* Employers know that most people take their problems with them. If you have a difficult relationship with your boss, find something positive about it. "He has helped me grow as a person. I'm a better manager than I was." Do not exaggerate about your boss's good qualities; you would not be looking for a change if your boss were truly wonderful.

3. What Are Your Business or Technical Skills?

You would think that your business or technical skills would be first on an interviewer's mind, but they're not. Your general attitude, your people skills, and your motivation are characteristics that rarely change and are difficult to instill. Business skills and specific industry knowledge are easily learned, making them less important. Even so, you may encounter some very direct questions to assess your business/technical knowledge. If you have done the research recommended in earlier chapters, you'll handle these questions like a pro.

a. What kinds of decisions are you responsible for on your current job? This question is designed to gain insight into your decision-making skills and to determine how decisive you are. Employers want to know whether you are a team player who makes decisions based on facts. They want to hire people who keep the company, coworkers, and subordinates in mind when making decisions. They also want to know the level of responsibility you have had. Be prepared to answer this question by giving it considerable thought beforehand. Think of one or two stories that illustrate participatory decisions and fast, decisive action.

b. What are your top priorities and how do you set priorities on the job? This question allows you to explain your responsibilities and your method for setting priorities. Tie your priority process to the mission and goals of the department or company. Illustrate your ability to keep a proper focus and not get lost in simply reacting to daily crises.

c. Tell me about a difficult problem you have had to deal with. Unfortunately, doing business means dealing with problems. Even a prospering business faces problems. This question is designed to understand your thought process. Analyze the method you generally use to deal with problems. Outline it so that you can show you do not just react to problems without conscious thought. For example, maybe you use a three-step process. First, you examine any problem by probing for cause, knowing that many crises are simply symptoms of a greater problem and that a quick fix of a symptom can cause even more trouble later. Second, once you have determined the cause, you assess whether it is your responsibility to take care of it. You respect the chain of command and the integrity of each department manager. If the problem has roots in another department, you enlist the help of management in that department to find a solution. Third, you formulate a solution using all available resources and recommend the solution to your boss or the appropriate responsible person.

As always, use a success story that demonstrates such a process.

4. What Is Your Attitude Toward Work and Life?

The interviewer is trying to determine how optimistic you are. Employers want to know if you have simply put on a happy face or whether you have a genuinely positive outlook. Honesty is important in this case, and a good attitude is, too. If you are using your win book, you truly can put forth a positive attitude.

a. What did you like most and what did you least like about your last company? This is not an opportunity to complain. Focus on the positive qualities of your last/current company. If you want to name a negative quality or explain your reason for leaving, present it in a positive way. "The opportunity for growth was limited because the company was too small." "I have discovered I'm interested in learning about different kinds of business. I believe the new knowledge will make me a better overall business person." Turn this question into an opportunity to compliment your prospective company rather than complain about your old job.

5. How Motivated Are You?

Unmotivated people are a dime a dozen. Self-motivated people are hard to find. Present yourself as a well-focused, highly self-motivated individual, and the job offers will come.

a. Where do you want to be in five years? The real purpose behind this question is to determine your goal orientation, and you want to be prepared with a safe answer. If it is your desire to become president of the company in five years, you may scare the person interviewing you. If you want a great job so you can retire early, the interviewer may think you lack motivation. Your best approach is to respond with a generic answer that shows motivation, such as: "I want to be known as an expert in my field and I want to be part of a winning team. I believe that actual promotions will take care of themselves if I focus on increasing my professional skills and making a significant contribution."

b. How do you feel about your career progress to date? Motivated people feel good about themselves. This is another question designed to assess your view of yourself. Be positive. As a career changer you may sometimes feel that you leaned your success ladder up against the wrong building. But remember, no matter what your former career, you gained skills that will lead you toward success in your next career of choice. Focus on the positive skills you have learned and tell the interviewer that you believe the best is yet to come.

Closing the Sale . . . Getting the Offer

Closing is the easiest part of the interview if you have worked the process effectively. If you have established your value by listening to the needs of the interviewer and demonstrating your ability to meet those needs, then the close is the logical conclusion to the process.

Always ask for the appropriate action. If the person you are talking with is not the final decision-maker, ask that your name be passed on to the next person in the process. If the interviewer is the decision-maker, ask them 1) when they expect to make the decision and 2) what criteria will be used to determine who will be hired.

The answer to the first question tells you their timing, thus reducing anxiety while you wait for a call. The answer to the second question allows you a chance to deal with job requirements that you may not have uncovered during the previous interviews. At this point, you may need to demonstrate an additional skill or reinforce the quality of your candidacy.

Finally, end the interview by saying that you want the job and will be expecting a call on the day they make their decision.

It isn't hard to be good at interviewing, it just takes practice. Your senior experience offers you the ability to find truly meaningful stories and then adapt those stories to the specific needs of the interviewer. Younger people don't have your experience. They cannot relate to the interviewing process as well as you can. Use these interviewing tips, teamed with your selling resume, and you'll sell yourself into a new career.

Chapter 13

There Is Life After Mid-Career Crisis

SUCCESSFULLY EMERGING from a mid-career crisis is not easy, but the rewards are well worth the effort. Compared to the alternative—hanging in a constant state of limbo, awash in depression and despair—there is no question that it is worth the struggle.

Everyone we know who has put real effort into a career transition has come back to report they feel proud and fulfilled. They have all felt better off than before the change, even if they earn less money in their new career.

A few of those we've known, like Clint, whom we mentioned in the first chapter, have returned to a career path similar to their original profession. Yet the journey through mid-career crisis gave them a new appreciation for and understanding of work and the workplace. They have been through the grass-is-greener delusion and now understand every job has its pluses and minuses.

Once you have journeyed through your mid-career crisis, you will have a new appreciation for those people, near and dear, who helped you cope. Your life will be full and rewarding. What you once viewed as a sunset will now be seen as a sunrise. This new optimism will be the engine that drives you to success in your mid-career change.

We've watched many people make successful mid-career changes using the information in this book. Before, you had the desire; now you have the tools.

Have fun, and best of luck.

Appendix A

Source Books of Company Names

Thomas Register. Thomas Publishing Co., 461 Eighth Avenue, New York, NY 10001. Lists 100,000 manufacturers by product and location.

National Trade and Professional Associations of the United States. Columbia Books, Inc., 1350 New York Avenue, N.W., Suite 207, Washington, DC 20005.

Directory of Personnel Consultants by Specialization (Industry Grouping). National Association of Personnel Consultants, Round House Square, 1432 Duke St., Alexandria, VA 22314.

Career Guide to Professional Associations. Garrett Park Press, Garrett Park, MD 20896.

Contacts Influential: Commerce and Industry Directory. Contacts Influential Market Research and Development Services, 321 Bush St., Suite 203, San Francisco, CA 94104. Sorted by industry and lists names of key personnel.

Encyclopedia of Associations. Gale Research, Inc., 835 Penobscot Building, Detroit, MI 48226. Lists nonprofit trade associations in the United States.

The books listed below are available in your local library.

Guide to American Directories. Contains complete information on 5,200 directories in 200 subjects.

Standard Rate & Data. Names and addresses of trade publications listed by topic.

Standard & Poor's Register of Corporations, Directories & Executives.

Dun & Bradstreet Million Dollar Directory. Lists major corporations by industry.

Appendix B

Entrepreneurs Resource List

Here is a list of a few resources that can provide you with more information about owning your own business.

- Small Business Administration: 1441 L Street N.W., Washington, DC 20416; (202) 653–6365 or (800) 827–5722. Also check the telephone book for a local office in your area.

- SCORE (Service Corps of Retired Executives): This agency is composed of retired volunteers who can give you advice about running or improving your business. Your local telephone directory should list an office or contact.

- Your chamber of commerce offers market research information and business directories. The chamber can also tell you about job training programs in which the government pays one-half of the employee's salary in exchange for the employer's training the person in a new skill. Check your local directory for chambers in your area.

- Check with your telephone company about business phones and Yellow Pages advertising. Check with AT&T, Sprint, or MCI about low-cost 800 service and the 800 business directory.

- Find out if your state has an economic development administration. If it does, this could be a valuable resource for information on financing, market research, partnerships, and small business "incubator" programs. Incubator programs team a business up with a number of professional state-paid consultants who can improve the management of the company.

- Check with your local community college to see what kind of business development programs it offers. You will probably find a number of cost-effective training programs that range from sales to finance.

- Ask the marketing department of your local university if it offers student intern programs. You may be able to use students to do marketing research for your business idea.

Appendix C

Top Ten Recruiting Firms

KORN/FERRY INTERNATIONAL
237 Park Ave.
New York, NY 10017

RUSSELL REYNOLDS ASSOCIATES,
INC.
200 Park Ave.
New York, NY 10167

HEIDRICK & STRUGGLES, INC.
245 Park Ave.
New York, NY 10167

SPENCER STUART & ASSOCIATES
55 E. 52nd St.
New York, NY 10055

PAUL R. RAY & CO., INC.
301 Commerce St.
Fort Worth, TX 76102

WARD HOWELL INTERNATIONAL,
INC.
99 Park Ave.
New York, NY 10016

LAMALIE ASSOCIATES
101 Park Ave.
New York, NY 10017

KEARNEY: EXECUTIVE SEARCH
222 S. Riverside Plaza
Chicago, IL 60606

EGON ZEHNDER INTERNATIONAL
55 E. 59th St.
New York, NY 10022

BOYDEN
260 Madison Ave.
New York, NY 10016

Index

About the Authors

JEAN RUSSELL NAVE began her professional career over twenty years ago. She gained sales and marketing management expertise while working for some of America's most successful companies, including Bank of America, Xerox Corporation, and Hewlett-Packard.

Currently she is president of Motivational Dynamics, Inc., a management training and consulting firm. This position has allowed her to work with prominent management authorities, among them Tom Peters and Ken Blanchard.

Jean's reputation as a career management consultant received regional recognition in 1984 with the publication of her first book, *Women . . . the World's Greatest Salesmen!* Jean has hosted two cable television shows in Portland, Oregon: "Traveling the Road of Success," a series of personal growth programs; and "Business Upbeat," a business news show. She also authored *The Quest for Real Success*, a book about values.

LOUISE M. NELSON graduated *cum laude* from Chico State University, California, with a degree in Social Science. Soon thereafter, she and her husband moved to Oregon. She started her career as a counselor with a private placement agency, and later entered the sales field, working for the world's largest business forms manufacturer. For ten years Louise excelled as a sales representative, receiving numerous awards, while continuing to act as a career consultant on the side.

In 1985 she and her husband formed a partnership and bought a printing company in Portland. The business was sold four years later after annual revenue had increased threefold. Since then, she has divided her time between writing and career consulting.